Key English Skills

About the Key English Skills Books

At Key Stage 2 (Years 3, 4, 5 and 6) (ages 7–11) your child will learn key English skills in speaking, listening, reading and writing.

These books contain activities designed to build your child's confidence in English as they progress from Years 3 to 6. They cover the skills your child is learning in school, including grammar, spelling and punctuation that will form the basis of the new tests at the end of Key Stage 2 (Year 6).

At the end of Key Stage 2 (Year 6), your child will sit National Curriculum tests in English. The English grammar, punctuation and spelling test will assess levels 3–5 of the Key Stage 2 National Curriculum programme of study for English. A separate level 6 test will be available for schools that wish to enter children who are expected to be working above level 5.

Your child's teacher will make a separate judgement on how well your child is doing in writing – such as composing letters or writing stories.

Key English Skills Ages 9–10

This book is divided into sets of manageable activities that give your child additional help with their reading and writing.

Reading practice – a text for your child to read followed by questions and related activities:
- Recognising and forming different tenses.
- Understanding grammatical structures.
- Looking for meaning beyond the literal.
- Using inference and deduction.

Writing practice – activities that focus on grammar and language, as well as a writing task:
- Using correct grammar, such as recognising and forming different tenses.
- Using punctuation – full stops, question marks, exclamation marks, commas, speech marks and apostrophes.
- Spelling, including the use of common prefixes and suffixes.
- Understanding the relevance of word families and the roots and origins of words.

How to Use this Book at Home

- Find a quiet, comfortable place to work, away from distractions.
- Encourage your child to work through all the questions in the book. Aim to work through one section per day or set up a regular time for completing the activities in the book.
- Make sure your child has extra pieces of paper or a separate notebook to write their answers on where necessary.
- When your child has finished working through the book, help them to check their answers using the **free downloadable answers** available on our website.
- Download the **free progress chart** available on our website, which allows you and your child to work out which skills can be improved upon.
- Go back to the areas your child found the most difficult and help them to work through the questions again. It might be beneficial to find your child some more practice material in these areas. Collins offers a wide range of English practice material for ages 5–11. See our website.

To download a free copy of the **answers** for this book, go to:
www.collinseducation.com/KESAnswers9-10

Contents

Reading	Chinese New Year	4
Activities		5
Proofreading		6
Grammar	Capital letters	7
Writing		8
Language	Using Words	9
Reading	The Snake	10
Activities		11
Cloze		12
Grammar	Nouns	13
Writing	Interesting Animals	14
Language	Masculine and Feminine Nouns	15
Reading	The Lobster	16
Activities		17
Proofreading		18
Grammar	Conjunctions	19
Writing	Fairy Tales	20
Language	Singular and Plural	21
Reading	The Strange Ship	22
Activities		23
Cloze		24
Grammar	Types of Nouns	25
Writing	Addressing an Envelope	26
Language	Prefixes	27
Reading	Nell and the Goose	28
Activities		29
Phonics	Fun with Words	30
Grammar	Pronouns	31
Writing	Short Stories	32
Language	Suffixes	33
Reading	The Conquest of Space	34
Activities		35
Proofreading		36
Grammar	Adjectives	37
Writing	How to Write a Letter	38
Language	Homonyms	39
Reading	The Magnificent Cave	40
Activities		41
Cloze		42
Grammar	Verbs	43
Writing	Visits	44
Language	Homes and Houses	45
Reading	Nanuk	46
Activities		47
Fun with Words		48
Grammar	Tenses	49
Writing	Adventures	50
Language	Participles	51

Reading	The Titanic	52
Activities		53
Cloze		54
Grammar	Adverbs	55
Writing	Suitable Endings	56
Language	Quotation Marks	57
Reading	The Burglar Who Called the Police	58
Activities		59
Fun with Words		60
Grammar	Adjectives and Adverbs	61
Writing	Reviews	62
Language		63
Reading	Gold	64
Activities		65
Cloze		66
Grammar	The Comma	67
Writing	Things That Make Me Mad	68
Language		69
Reading	Mysteries of Migration	70
Activities		71
Cloze		72
Grammar	The Apostrophe (')	73
Writing	Friendships	74
Language		75
Reading	The Enchanted Stag	76
Activities		77
Fun with Words		78
Grammar	Contractions	79
Writing	Newspapers	80
Language	Abbreviations	81
Reading	The Submarine	82
Activities		83
Cloze		84
Grammar	Conjunctions	85
Writing	Complete the Stories	86
Language		87
Reading	William Tell	88
Activities		89
Cloze	Radar	90
Grammar	Prepositions	91
Writing	Conversations	92
Language	'Then' – Overused Word	93
Grammar	Revision	94
Language	'Got' – Overused Word	95
Language	Silent Letters	96

Reading

 A Read the text.

Chinese New Year

The Chinese New Year is the most important festival not only in China, but also for millions of Chinese people living around the world. The Chinese use a lunar calendar, based on the changing phases of the Moon. Because of this, Chinese New Year falls on a different date each year, but it usually takes place in January or February.

Getting ready for the New Year involves cleaning the house, buying new clothes and putting up New Year decorations. New Year's Eve dinner is the biggest meal of the year, and many of the dishes have a *symbolic* meaning. For example, the dumplings which are eaten represent wealth, because they are similar in shape to ancient Chinese gold or silver *ingots*.

As soon as the New Year arrives, firecrackers are set off. Red packets (which are simply red envelopes with money in) are exchanged. Giving someone a red packet is a way of wishing them good luck and wealth for the coming year. Dragon dancing is another custom associated with Chinese New Year. The Lantern Festival, which takes place on the first full Moon of the year, marks the end of the two-week long New Year celebrations.

No one really knows the *origins* of the New Year celebrations in China, but legend has it that a beast called Nian appeared every year at the same time and ate people, until a wise old man found a way to stop it. The grateful people began celebrating the anniversary of the beast's *defeat*.

Every Chinese year is named after one of twelve animals: rat, ox, tiger, rabbit, dragon, snake, horse, ram, monkey, rooster, dog or pig. The Chinese believe that your personality is influenced by the animal in whose year you are born.

4

Activities

A **Answer these questions.**

1. What is a lunar calendar?
2. When does Chinese New Year take place?
3. Name two things which people do in preparation for the Chinese New Year.
4. What do the dumplings at the New Year's Eve meal represent and why?
5. Why are red packets exchanged?
6. Which festival concludes the New Year Celebrations?
7. Explain the legend behind Chinese New Year in your own words.
8. If you could choose one of the twelve animals associated with the Chinese calendar, which would you choose and why?

B **Look up the words in *italics* in your dictionary. Write an interesting sentence for each one.**

C **Summarise the text in your own words. Use about 10 sentences.**

D **Write the sentences using to, two or too.**

1. David is _____ ill _____ go _____ the pop concert.
2. The last _____ days were _____ wet _____ play games.
3. The teacher told me _____ leave for home at _____ o'clock.
4. Prasad went _____ the dance and Satira went with _____ of her friends.
5. My _____ sisters travel _____ school by bus.
6. I am going _____ the film today with my _____ cousins.
7. I am _____ young _____ be admitted _____ the dance.
8. It is _____ early _____ retire _____ bed.
9. The question was _____ hard _____ answer.
10. It is _____ soon after dinner _____ go swimming.
11. The teacher ordered _____ of us _____ play in the game.
12. If you are going _____ the pop concert may I come _____?
13. The _____ of us were _____ tired _____ play in the garden.
14. The teacher showed the pupils _____ ways _____ solve the problem.

Proofreading

 Correct the mistakes in this story.

The Sick Lion

Once, a lion bekame sick in His lair and many of the uther animels came to visit him.

However, the fox never kame, and finally the lion wrote a long letter too him, reminding the fox of there friendship and suggesting that he come and visit the lion's lare.

The fox was in the loccality one Day, but after sum thought he went home without seeing the lion and write a letter insted. He said that he was sorrey to here that the lion was ill and he promisd that he would say lot's off prayers for his recoviry. "But I cannot see my way to visit you now," He wrote.

"Because while I saw lots off footprints goin into your den, I saw nun coming out again."

Grammar

Capital Letters

> We use capital letters:
> - At the beginning of a sentence.
> - For the letter "I".
> - For the names and titles of people, e.g. Dr Mary Smith.
> - For the names of places, months of the year, days of the week and special days.
> - For titles of things, e.g. Robinson Crusoe, Jaws.

 Insert the capital letters and full stops.

it was a gorgeous sunny saturday in the middle of july we decided that it would be a great idea to have a barbecue we invited mr and mrs Jones and their daughter, natalie we invited mr willis and his son, jake naturally we invited uncle toby as well.

by six o'clock that evening we were all starving mum was tending the charcoal dad was putting some finishing touches to the kebabs, burgers and chicken legs uncle toby and the rest of the guests had arrived we hadn't seen uncle toby since april so we had a lot of catching up to do

by half past six the smell of the meat being barbecued was making my knees go weak the aroma was teasing my nostrils it was difficult not to just grab a chicken leg and run however, i managed to control myself and soon we were all tucking into food that was every bit as good as it smelt

 Insert the capital letters where needed.

1. i am going to the film with George.
2. lille is an industrial city in northern France.
3. mrs flood went to London and bought a dress in Harrods.
4. the president of the united states of america lives in the white house.
5. the first of april is called "fool's" day.
6. maha is my cousin and she lives in kinshasa.
7. every tuesday in june she visits her aunt hannah.
8. the bangladeshi team should win on saturday.
9. last sunday I visited my aunt erina.

 Rewrite using fewer 'ands' and more full stops.

It was a crisp winter's morning and I jumped out of bed and dressed quickly. Today we were going to visit our cousins in Manchester and I hurried downstairs and found everyone was waiting for me. Without further delay, I ran to the car and got in and Dad started the engine and we were on our way.

7

Writing

A **Copy this passage, filling in the blanks.**

My name is _____. My friends call me _____. I am _____ years of age. I have _____ eyes and _____ hair. My height is _____ and my weight is _____. I live in _____ with my _____. I have _____ brothers and _____ sisters. I like to play _____ with my friends after _____. My favourite hobby is _____. I have a fine collection of _____. I should like very much to be _____ when I grow up.

B **Write a list of your:**

1. 5 favourite foods.
2. 5 favourite drinks.
3. 5 favourite films.
4. 5 favourite books.
5. 5 favourite actors/actresses.
6. 5 favourite TV programmes.
7. 5 favourite pop groups/singers.

C **Write a description of your best friend. Remember to mention: age, height, likes, dislikes, colour of hair and eyes, dress, habits.**

_____
_____
_____
_____
_____

D **Write a yearly diary. Include each year from your year of birth. Example: 1999: Born in Dubai.**

E **Write a diary for one day.**

_____
_____
_____
_____
_____

8

Language

Using Words

A Write **a** or **an**.

1. The girl ate _____ egg and _____ sausage for her breakfast.
2. My brother saw _____ fox and _____ eagle in the forest.
3. I saw _____ aeroplane disappear behind _____ white cloud.
4. The carpenter had _____ axe and _____ saw in his hand.
5. She gave the boy _____ apple and _____ orange.
6. My sister Aditi is _____ actress and my sister Erina is _____ model.
7. I have _____ uncle and _____ aunt in New York.
8. The waitress wore _____ apron and _____ white cap.
9. _____ ant and _____ flea are two tiny insects.
10. The gardener planted _____ elm tree and _____ oak tree in the garden.
11. She gave the lady _____ rose and _____ orchid.
12. _____ ewe is _____ young sheep.
13. _____ axe is _____ useful weapon.
14. _____ onion is bigger than _____ pea.
15. _____ ugly earwig crawled under _____ mossy stone.
16. I have _____ yellow canary and _____ tame rabbit.
17. John saw _____ otter and _____ beaver near the big dam.
18. Meera saw _____ unusual animal and _____ enormous elephant in the zoo.
19. _____ hour later I visited _____ ancient castle.
20. _____ apricot is smaller than _____ cucumber.
21. _____ eulogy was given at the graveside.
22. _____ ostrich and _____ albatross are two large birds.

B Write the words.

			I	S	T		Someone who types.
			I	S	T		Someone who sketches pictures.
				I	S	T	Someone who extracts teeth.
				I	S	T	Someone who rides a bicycle.
				I	S	T	Someone who goes on holidays to other countries.
				I	S	T	Someone who works in a pharmacy.
				I	S	T	Someone who sells flowers.
					I	S	T	Someone who drives a car.
				I	S	T		Someone who studies plants.
					I	S	T	Someone who writes for the newspapers.

C Dictionary fun. Write five words that include these letters.

1. ant (e.g. elephant)
2. oil _____
3. ore _____
4. all _____
5. our _____
6. ful _____
7. full _____
8. ous _____
9. ment _____
10. ion _____

9

Reading

 A Read the story.

The Snake

On another day, as we were going back to the camp in the evening, Toto had wandered some ten metres in front of me, when suddenly a small snake slid out from behind a stone, passed right in front of Toto, and dropped into a crack between two rocks. Toto yelled with terror, then ran back to me, and stood, with his teeth chattering, holding his hand as if to show where he had been bitten.

I examined it carefully, but could not see the tiny mark that would have been made by the snake's fangs. I made sure of this, and then told Toto that he was only frightened, and that the snake had not touched him. He did not believe me. He had been so scared by the sudden sight of the snake that he was certain that he was hurt and probably imagined that he was going to die. Knowing that this was not so, I tried to *coax* him to come back with me to camp. He would not come.

I walked ahead, expecting him to follow. After a few paces, I looked back and saw the little fellow stretched out on the ground, convinced that he was too ill to move, and looking at me with *piteous entreaty* not to leave him. So I picked him up and carried him to my tent, where at last the sight of a bunch of bananas *distracted* his thoughts until he forgot his terror, and half an hour later he was sitting on my bed, playing as *contentedly* as ever.

Activities

A **Answer these questions. (Answer them in sentence form where possible.)**

1. Was Toto a dog, a boy, or a monkey? Give a reason for your answer.
2. What was it that frightened Toto?
3. How did Toto show his fear?
4. "I made sure of this" – he made sure of what, and how did he do it?
5. "He did not believe me" – what was it that he did not believe?
6. "After a few paces, I looked back" – what did the writer see when he looked back?
7. Why did he have to carry Toto back to the tent?
8. Explain: his teeth chattered; distracted his thoughts; the snake's fangs; piteous entreaty.
9. "Toto had wandered … in front of me". Write two sentences of your own, one of which will contain the word "wandered", and another, the word "wondered".
10. Toto was "scared"; "terrified"; "frightened". Which of these words suggests the least degree of fear?
11. What is the past tense of these verbs: forget; bite; sit; hold; try; come; drop?

B **Look up the words in *italics* in your dictionary. Write an interesting sentence for each one.**

C **Summarise the story in your own words. Use about 10 sentences.**

D **Rewrite the phrases using the correct descriptive words.**

| blare   ring   dripping   trickle   call   clatter   crack   clanking |
| booming   clink   creak   bang   murmur   crackling |

1. the _____ of a stream
2. the _____ of a drum
3. the _____ of a trumpet
4. the _____ of a gun
5. the _____ of a telephone
6. the _____ of a bugle
7. the _____ of an engine
8. the _____ of chains
9. the _____ of hooves
10. the _____ of coins
11. the _____ of wood
12. the _____ of a whip
13. the _____ of a hinge
14. the _____ of water

11

Cloze

A cloze text is a text with words missing. You need to replace the missing words.

A Write the missing words.

called   horses   breeds   toes   America   first   meat   bigger
years   about   their   until   America   out   that   are   changing

Millions of _____ ago, small animals no bigger than foxes ran _____ the forests of North _____. They were like tiny ponies, except _____ they had four toes and they were _____ 'dawn horses'. These little animals kept _____ over the years. They grew bigger and _____ and their _____ grew fewer _____ they had only one, now called a hoof. Then a strange thing happened, all the horses in _____ died _____. It was the Spaniards who first brought horses back to America. In the stone age there were wild _____ in Ireland. When these horses were _____ tamed, they were kept for their _____ and _____ milk but very soon they were carrying heavy loads. Nowadays, there _____ many different _____ of horse.

B Write the missing words.

water   seconds   size   cycle   means   less   vapour   down

A piece of South American rainforest, the _____ of a football pitch, is cut _____ every three _____. Trees 'breathe out' _____ vapour which is turned into rain in the water _____. Destroying these rainforests _____ that less water _____ is made and _____ rain falls.

12

Grammar

Nouns

> **Nouns are naming words. They name people, places, things and animals.**

 Write the nouns.

1. A plague of locusts ate all the wheat.
2. The girl chopped wood for the fire.
3. The Czar of Russia had great wealth.
4. Rabbits eat grass, but otters eat fish.
5. We breathe air into our lungs.
6. The fisherman filled his basket with fish.
7. A pack of hungry dogs attacked the sheep.
8. The owner of the hotel is a wealthy lady.
9. Joan kept her parrot in a cage.
10. The ship struck a reef, but the crew was saved.

B Find the 28 nouns.

It was a glorious September day, with the warm sun shining brightly in the blue sky. High up in the air, the lark was filling the heavens with melody, and from tree and hedge came the sweet notes of thrush, blackbird and robin. The sheep were lying peacefully in the shade of the trees, and the horses were knee-deep in the river. Down in the valley, the machines were noisily cutting the golden corn; but louder than the noise of the machines were the shouts of the children bathing in the cool pool by the ash grove.

 Write suitable nouns.

1. The girl limped home as her _____ was injured.
2. There was an interesting _____ on the radio.
3. The photographer put a _____ in her _____.
4. The rider fell off his _____.
5. I witnessed a collision of two _____.
6. The motorist put _____ in the car.
7. I was bitten by a _____ in the woods.
8. He put some _____ on his bread.

13

Writing

Interesting Animals

Write an interesting paragraph about each of the following animals. Some helpful words are given.

 Giraffe

Africa
lovely, gentle animal
tallest animal
long, slender neck
spotted body
feeds on tender leaves

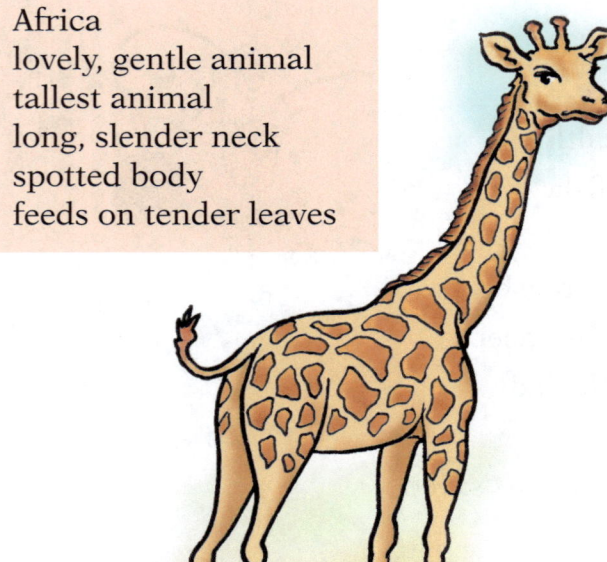

 Kangaroo

Australia
strong hind legs
thick, powerful tail
leaps and bounds
pouch for its young
feeds on grass

 Lion

the cat family
king of the beasts
roars and prowls
tawny mane
powerful jaws and teeth

 Seal

lives on land and sea
waddles clumsily
devours fish
flippers
sharp teeth

Language

Masculine and Feminine Nouns

> Man is masculine Woman is feminine
> Boy is masculine Girl is feminine

 A Divide these words into two lists – feminine and masculine.

manageress	uncle	son
actor	mother	princess
Ms	manager	daughter
king	brother	prince
sister	father	nephew
actress	Sir	hero
aunt	bride	niece
Mr	Madam	heroine
queen	groom	

 B Underline the feminine words.

1. The princess greeted the actress.
2. The headmistress has a daughter in my class.
3. Her niece is a famous woman.
4. My grandmother was a great athlete when she was young.
5. The landlady is a spinster.
6. The waitress gave her a fright.
7. The woman thanked her hostess.
8. The bride waved to her sister.
9. The manageress gave instructions to the stewardess.
10. The shepherdess searched for the lost ewe.

 C Underline the masculine words.

1. Father and uncle were laughing.
2. The prince spoke to the king.
3. The man wore his new hat.
4. The husband went to see his friend.
5. My brother waved to Louis.
6. The hero thanked the steward for his help.
7. The count greeted the duke.
8. The man handed his son a cheque.
9. The boy spoke to the manager.
10. The waiter served Mr Carroll.

Reading

 A Read the text.

The Lobster

Lobsters have lived in the sea for millions of years. These shellfish crawl around the ocean floor on slender legs. They are protected by their strong shells.

The lobster lives in *shallow* waters around our coasts. Just like the fish, it breathes through tiny blood vessels in its gills. Its long feelers help it find food among the rocks and seaweed. At night it hunts for dead fish, shellfish, snails and water insects. The hungry lobster will even *devour* its brother or sister. If it loses a claw or a leg, it grows a new one. What a strange creature!

The female lobster cleverly glues her eggs to the underside of her body. She carries them with her until they are hatched. Many of the baby lobsters are eaten by the bigger fish. Those that escape hide among the rocks or bury themselves deep in the sand. There they grow big and strong. Each summer they are fitted with a new suit of *armour* and a fresh stomach lining. They hide in a dark hole until the new crusty shell hardens.

Fishermen catch lobsters in funnel-shaped pots. A piece of fish is used as *bait*. Once a lobster crawls into a pot, it is trapped.

Lobster is one of the world's favourite seafoods.

Activities

A Answer these questions.

1. Where does the lobster live?
2. How does the lobster move?
3. How does it protect itself?
4. What foods does it eat?
5. Where does the female lobster carry her eggs?
6. How does the lobster breathe?
7. What dangers await the baby lobsters?
8. How do fishermen trap lobsters?
9. What do you think is strange about the lobster?
10. Have you ever seen a lobster in real life?

B Look up the words in *italics* in your dictionary. Write an interesting sentence for each one.

C Summarise the text in your own words. Use about 10 sentences.

D Write the sentences using **is** or **are**.

1. Her hands _____ clean but her face _____ dirty.
2. My gloves _____ upstairs and my coat _____ in the hall.
3. His cheeks _____ swollen and his nose _____ cut.
4. The boy's feet _____ cold but his hands _____ warm.
5. Her eye _____ sore and her tooth _____ loose.
6. Aba's face _____ pale and her ears _____ red.
7. Her fingers _____ swollen and her thumb _____ broken.
8. When she _____ singing what _____ you doing?
9. The stranger's eyes _____ brown and her hair _____ jet black.
10. John _____ crying because his teeth _____ broken.

17

Proofreading

  Correct the mistakes in this story.

A Father and his Sons

Once, a hard-working farther had a family of sons. the sons were verry troubuesome and were alays quarrlling amung themselves.

The father was very worried about this, and one day h gathered the hole family around him. He showd them a bondle o sticks, tied together with cord.

"I want each of you to take this bondle in his hands," he said, "an try with all your strength to break it."

Beginnning with the youngest, each boy tried in turn too break the sticks, but none sucseeded.

"Now, untie the bundle," said the amuzed father, "hnd see what you can do with peach twig."

They did so, and with great eas, each of them snapped the single sticks to peeces.

"I have a bit of advize for you now," explained the father. "Keep together as a family and you are safe. Divide, and you are in truble."

Grammar

Conjunctions

> A conjunction is a word used to join small sentences together.
> Example: We have missed the bus so we will have to walk.

A **Find the conjunctions.**

We could not get into the house because we had left the keys on the hall table. We would have to wait outside in the garden until my brother came home at six o'clock. Chris thought he could climb in through the bedroom window although this was not a good plan because we didn't have a long enough ladder.

B **Write the missing conjunctions.**

1. We went to the zoo _____ saw some elephants.
2. Lucy was wet _____ she had forgotten her umbrella.
3. I like coffee _____ I would prefer tea.
4. Baldev put on his suit _____ he went to work.
5. You cannot go in the sea _____ you can swim.

| before |
| and |
| because |
| unless |
| but |

C **Fill the blanks with conjunctions.**

We were locked out _____ we had lost our keys. Mum was at Grandma's house _____ she would come home early _____ we could phone her and let her know. We could not phone _____ Mrs Jones next door was at home. We went to ask if we could call Mum from her house. We rang the bell _____ Mrs Jones called out telling us to wait _____ she was having a bath. We were waiting on the doorstep _____ Dad came home early. He was not very pleased _____ moaned at us, "_____ you start looking after your things better you will have to go to Gran's every night."

Writing

Fairy Tales

A Do you know the story of *Jack and the Beanstalk*?
Write a different ending.
Start with Jack running out of the giant's house.

B Write a different ending to the story of *Red Riding Hood*.
Start from her entering Grandma's cottage.

C Pick your favourite fairy tale. Write the story from a different viewpoint.

Language

Singular and Plural

If you are in doubt about any of the answers, please check your dictionary.

A Write these sentences in the plural.

1. The boy worked in the city.
2. The goose was killed by the fox.
3. The hero saved the lady.
4. The thief stole the ruby.
5. The mouse ate the cheese.
6. The army dug the trench.
7. The man chased the donkey.
8. The wolf devoured the sheep.
9. The horse hurt its hoof.
10. The tomato in the box is rotten.

B Write these sentences in the singular.

1. The women picked the tomatoes.
2. The flies landed on the bushes.
3. The men are afraid of the women.
4. The thieves stole the watches.
5. The donkeys had sore hooves.
6. The dwarves lived in the valleys.
7. The children picked the leaves.
8. The dishes were on the shelves.
9. The mice lived in the pianos.
10. The potatoes were the same size as the oranges.

C Write these sentences in the plural.

1. The man captured the robber.
2. The woman sang some songs.
3. The fisherman caught a trout and a salmon.
4. The shepherd watched over his flock.
5. The knife is on the shelf.
6. The lady gave a present to the child.
7. The farmer felled the tree in the field.
8. The mouse escaped from the trap.
9. The potato was too big to cook with the tomato.
10. The thief stole the watch.
11. The wolf killed the sheep.
12. The fox attacked the goose.
13. The man ate the trout.
14. The woman screamed when the mouse appeared.

21

Reading

 A Read the story.

The Strange Ship

As Captain Morehouse climbed up onto the deck of the Dei Gratia, on the morning of the 8th of December, 1872, little did he realise that one of the greatest mystery stories of all time was about to unfold before his eyes. Thankfully the Atlantic crossing had been smooth and uneventful, and the Dei Gratia was now less than three hundred kilometres from her *destination*, Gibraltar. The quiet thoughts of the captain were suddenly interrupted by eager cries of "ship ahoy! ship ahoy!" – one of the crew had spotted a ship coming towards them on the starboard side. Quickly snatching his telescope, Morehouse soon *observed* that there was something strange about this ship, for she was steering wildly and lurching through the waves. And what was even more disconcerting, nobody appeared to be on deck! The alarmed captain immediately sent four of his men out by rowing boat to board the ship and investigate. A search of the ship confirmed that there was not a single soul aboard. The ship was the Marie Celeste which had set sail from New York a month earlier.

No clue could be found as to the crew's disappearance. There was plenty of food and water aboard; all the crew's belongings were neatly packed in their sea chests; and furthermore, there was no sign of any violence having taken place. When Captain Morehouse sailed into Gibraltar with the Marie Celeste, it caused a *sensation*, and a full *enquiry* was ordered without delay. Did the crew mutiny? Were they attacked by pirates? Was some mysterious illness responsible for their disappearance? Or could a giant sea monster have swept them all overboard?

These and many other questions were asked, but no conclusive answer was ever found to explain the mystery of the Marie Celeste.

Activities

A **Answer these questions. (Answer in sentence form where possible.)**

1. Where was Captain Morehouse on the morning of the 8th December, 1872?
2. What was the destination of the Dei Gratia and how many more kilometres did she have to travel?
3. How were the captain's thoughts interrupted?
4. What alarmed Captain Morehouse about the ship he saw?
5. Describe what action he took in order to investigate the ship.
6. What was the name of the ship, and from where did she come?
7. Pretend you are one of the sailors sent to investigate the ship. Describe what you saw when you went on board.
8. What happened when the captain sailed into Gibraltar with the Marie Celeste?
9. Write your own ideas or theory as to what must have happened to the crew of the Marie Celeste.
10. Find out the meaning of these words: starboard; lurching; disconcerting; conclusive.
11. Write each of the above words in a sentence of your own.

B **Look up the words in *italics* in your dictionary. Write an interesting sentence for each one.**

C **Summarise the story in your own words. Use about 10 sentences.**

D **Write the sentences using I or me.**

1. He pushed _____ and _____ fell into the pool.
2. She gave _____ a pear and _____ ate it.
3. The teacher asked _____ to read the book and _____ did so willingly.
4. She and _____ played the guitar.
5. The dog chased _____ and _____ jumped over the ditch.
6. The teacher told _____ to go home and _____ was delighted.
7. Mina divided the sweets between Sujit and _____.
8. Amira is older than _____ but _____ am taller than her.
9. The ball dropped between Peter and _____ but _____ got it.
10. She gave _____ an orange and _____ bought her an apple.

23

Cloze

A Write the missing words.

> built made storeys under subside tilting Italy

The famous Tower of Pisa is the bell tower of the cathedral in Pisa, __Italy__. When it was only half __built__ (it was started in 1173), the soil __tilting__ one half began to __subside__, and the tower tipped. The tower is __made__ of white marble and has eight __storeys__. Engineers have managed to prevent any further __under__.

B Write the missing words.

> not spins silky doesn't gets moths across walks when own caught

WHY DOESN'T A SPIDER GET STUCK IN ITS OWN WEB?

A spider _____ two kinds of _____ thread out of its _____ body, and it uses both kinds _____ it makes a web. One kind is sticky. Flies, _____ and other insects get _____ in it. The other kind is _____ sticky. The spider _____ on threads of non-sticky silk when it runs _____ its web. The poor fly, of course, _____ know the difference and _____ caught.

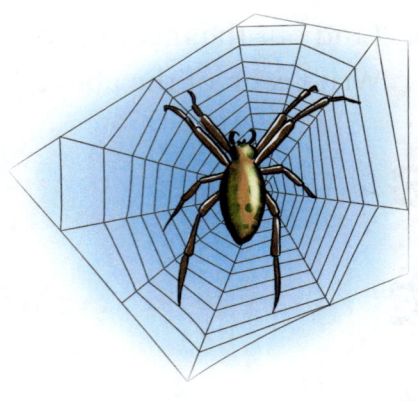

C Write the missing words.

> attacked scraps have liked animal rarely its

The hyena is not __its__ by either men or beasts. This __animal__ is so cowardly that it _____ defends itself when __attacked__. It seldom attacks and kills for __scraps__ food, but lives on _____ that other animals _____ left.

24

Grammar

Types of Nouns

> Nouns are names.
> Common nouns are names of things: girl, city, month, car, house.
> Proper nouns are names of people, animals, places, dates, brand names and titles: John, Goldie, The Mill House, London, April, Saab, the Bible.

 A Underline the common nouns in this passage and circle the proper nouns.

The sun had barely risen when we set out for the lake. Mum had made sandwiches for us and we were going to spend the day fishing. John had bought a new rod and he was anxious to use it. When we reached the lake we attached the motor to the boat and set off. During the day we would probably visit one of the many islands which dotted the lake.

 B Underline the proper nouns.

1. Rover the dog swam across the wide river.
2. Fluffy was playing happily with a ball of wool.
3. Sam enjoyed going to Lima.
4. A truck towed the broken-down Ford car along the road.
5. Sean Connery appeared in many films as British spy James Bond.
6. We went to Karachi to visit Aunt Hana.
7. Jan and Mia saw Mr Singh catch the thief.
8. The lion escaped from its cage in Shanghai Zoo.
9. Mrs Pierce shouted loudly at the barking dog.
10. Old Jock walked slowly along West Street.

 C Write four nouns for each group.

Group	Nouns			
dogs				
countries				
vegetables				
cities				
toys				
insects				
fruit				
flowers				
sports				
farm animals				

Writing

Addressing an Envelope

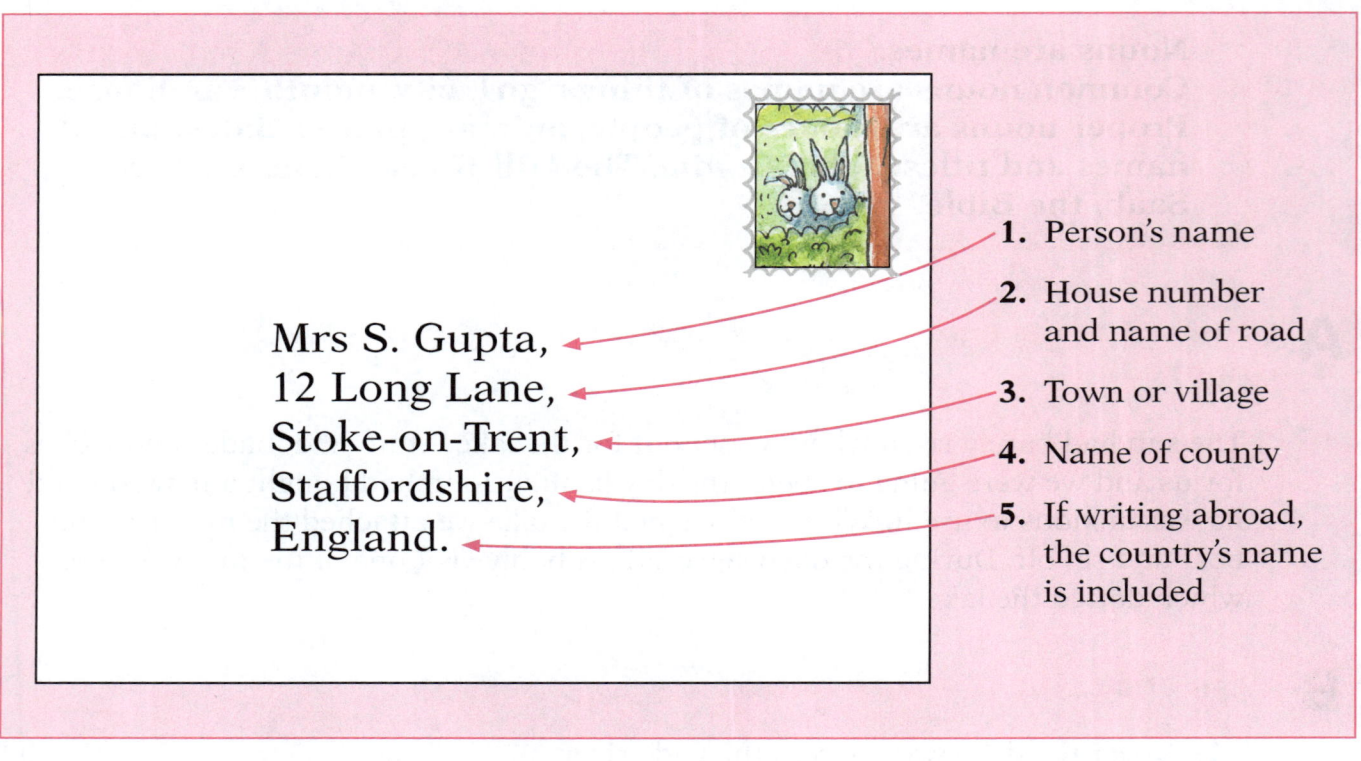

1. Person's name
2. House number and name of road
3. Town or village
4. Name of county
5. If writing abroad, the country's name is included

A Can you write what these abbreviations mean? There isn't a full point if the first and last letters of the complete word are included.

1. Rd _____
2. Ave _____
3. Sq. _____
4. Gdns _____
5. Co. _____
6. Tce _____
7. Cl. _____
8. Dr. _____

B Write your own name and address on this envelope. Do not forget the capital letters. Make sure you use commas and the full stop correctly.

26

Prefixes

Language

> A prefix is added to the beginning of a word to change its meaning.
> Example: ex is a prefix meaning out.

A Look at each picture below. Write a sentence to explain what is happening in the picture.

exhaust · excavate · extract
export · exit · expel

B Write one of the following prefixes for each of the words below:

1. _____ national
2. _____ build
3. _____ cast
4. _____ human
5. _____ take
6. _____ usual
7. _____ gone
8. _____ side
9. _____ judge
10. _____ roll

re-
un-
mis-
inter-
in-
fore-

C Add **un-** to the beginning of the following words and write a sentence for each.

1. _____ willing
2. _____ known
3. _____ kind
4. _____ reliable
5. _____ beaten
6. _____ fair
7. _____ cover
8. _____ lock
9. _____ true

D Write the opposite of these words by adding a prefix.

1. correct
2. safe
3. obey
4. direct
5. modest
6. loyal
7. aware
8. connect
9. possible
10. order
11. approve
12. regular
13. tidy
14. patient
15. clean

E Find a word in your dictionary with each prefix below:
vice, trans, de, ante, inter, sub, post, bi, ob, ab.

27

Reading

 A Read the story.

Nell and the Goose

Nell was disturbed at the thought of the man she had come so far to see, for she had heard frightening stories about him on her way to the lighthouse. Yet, she was *anxious* to see him, for she had been told by more than one person in this land of swamps that Meldon, the rough giant who was the chief keeper in the lighthouse, *possessed* a magic power of healing injured things. She knew, too, that the fowlers hated him because he interfered with their sport, but even so, her fear was *conquered* by the hope in her childish heart that he would heal what she carried in her arms.

She had never seen Meldon, and all but fled in panic at the apparition which almost filled the doorway immediately as she knocked – a huge man with jet-black hair and beard, prominent hump and crooked, claw-like hand. She edged timidly forward and held out what she had been carrying – a large, white bird. There were blood stains on her frock and on the wings of the bird which lay quite still.

Meldon carried the bird into the house and gently placed it on a table where it moved *feebly*. Nell's *curiosity* drove her in and she found herself in a warm room with a bright coal fire. The walls were covered with coloured pictures, and there was a pleasant, if unusual, smell.

The bird fluttered slightly when Meldon, with his good hand, carefully opened out its immense, white wings. The man seemed puzzled and looked inquiringly at the child. "Where did you find this bird?" he asked.
"In the marsh near our house, sir, where the fowlers were shooting this morning. What is it?"
"A snow goose from Canada."

28

Activities

A Answer these questions. (Answer in sentence form where possible.)

1. Why was Nell disturbed?
2. Why didn't the fowlers like Meldon?
3. What helped Nell to overcome her fear?
4. Why did Nell edge "timidly forward"?
5. How did the blood stains happen to be on Nell's frock?
6. Why did the bird remain so still?
7. Why was Nell so curious?
8. What do you think had happened to the bird?
9. Explain the following words: magic; fowlers; apparition; prominent; fluttered; inquiringly.
10. Write each of the above words in a sentence of your own.

B Look up the words in *italics* in your dictionary. Write an interesting sentence for each one.

C Summarise the story in your own words. Use about 10 sentences.

D Write the sayings using the correct word.

| fast | meek | swift | poor | quick | clear | white | busy | pale | strong | heavy |
| old | black | brown | silent | clean | soft | fresh | graceful | hungry | | |

1. as _____ as the hills
2. as _____ as a hare
3. as _____ as coal
4. as _____ as lead
5. as _____ as a lamb
6. as _____ as an ox
7. as _____ as a deer
8. as _____ as a wolf
9. as _____ as a swan
10. as _____ as a church mouse
11. as _____ as water
12. as _____ as death
13. as _____ as lightning
14. as _____ as a new pin
15. as _____ as crystal
16. as _____ as the grave
17. as _____ as a sheet
18. as _____ as an ant
19. as _____ as a berry
20. as _____ as putty

29

Phonics

Fun with Words

A There is only one correct spelling in each line. Can you write the correct spelling of the other two?

1. Strech, fractur, fourth   _____
2. Imposible, jostel, journey _____
3. Laughtir, luxery, monthly   _____
4. Arctic, Olympick, piller   _____
5. Rowdey, scoop, shortin   _____
6. Slippery, steadey, startel _____
7. Vacume, voluntery, wafer   _____
8. Sheikh, beleive, recieve   _____
9. Populer, postege, porridge _____
10. Commotion, caskit, biscuite _____

B How many vegetables and salad items can you find in the wordsearch? They can read in any direction. Challenge a friend.

b	o	c	y	e	k	s	r	a	p	c	a
c	b	p	n	b	p	p	c	e	e	p	r
p	b	a	o	p	c	c	g	r	a	m	s
p	e	c	i	b	c	a	b	c	a	b	i
b	e	b	n	c	b	r	m	r	o	e	l
r	t	c	o	b	b	r	r	r	c	o	o
e	r	b	a	b	c	o	c	u	a	l	c
p	o	c	c	p	w	t	t	p	e	r	c
p	o	c	t	b	t	t	o	e	o	c	o
e	t	t	p	t	e	b	k	c	e	f	r
p	e	p	e	l	s	w	e	d	e	c	b
e	p	l	c	r	e	b	m	u	c	u	c

C Write the words with **oo**.

1. __oo__   A silly person.
2. __oo__   Midday.
3. __oo__   The opposite of "rich".
4. __oo__   Worn by a sheep.
5. __oo__   Dirt from the chimney.
6. __oo__   It shines at night.
7. __oo__   Stolen goods.
8. __oo__   A hen's house.
9. __oo__   Worn on the foot.
10. __oo__ He prepares meals.
11. __oo__ A place for swimming.
12. __oo__ Part of a plant under the ground.

Grammar

Pronouns

> A pronoun is used in place of a noun.
> Example: *Carla* is always smiling. *She* is always smiling.
> Did *Hari* enjoy *the meal*? Did *he* enjoy *it*?

A Find the pronouns.

Eventually, the train pulled out of the station. I leaned out of the carriage window and began to wave. Jan was running along the platform. She was smiling but I knew there were tears in her eyes. I waved until she was only a blob in the distance. I knew I might never see her again but I wouldn't think of that now. A whole new world was opening up before me and there was no going back. I had come too far.

B Write the missing pronouns.

1. The woman travelled to Singapore but _____ lost her way.
2. The girl will listen to her father because she respects _____.
3. Have you found an apple as I lost _____?
4. My coat is light but _____ is warm.
5. Apples are good for you so you should eat _____.
6. Are you the boy _____ won the race?
7. Is that the car _____ crashed near the school?
8. I know nothing about _____.
9. It will be a secret between you and _____.
10. He is as tall as _____ am.

C Write these pronouns in alphabetical order.

1. mine, your, me, yours, my, I, you.

   _____

2. he, she, it, him, her, his, hers, its.

   _____

3. we, us, our, ours.

   _____

4. they, them, their, theirs.

   _____

Writing

Short Stories

Write a short story on each of the following titles. Use the help words.

 The accident

overslept   hurriedly dressed   snatched a quick breakfast   desperate hurry
dashing across the street   screeching of brakes   car skidded
struck a glancing blow   dazed   ambulance siren   stretcher
injuries not serious.

 Voyage into space

astronaut   space mission to   tearful farewell   launch site
strapped firmly inside   countdown   terrific surge of power   lift off
capsule window.

 An encounter with a shark

swimming   warm sea   shoals of fish   snorkelling   sudden shriek of horror
a shark fin   came closer   panic stricken   swam for our lives.

32

Language

Suffixes

> A suffix is a group of letters added to the end of a word to give a new word.
> Examples: self**ish**, publish**er**, teach**er**, harm**less**.

A Write two words for each suffix below.

1. -ous _____
2. -et _____
3. -ory _____
4. -er _____
5. -ist _____
6. -ence _____
7. -ance _____
8. -less _____
9. -ful _____
10. -eer _____
11. -ier _____
12. -fly _____
13. -ant _____
14. -ible _____

B Add -less to the end of the following words and write a sentence for each.

1. care
2. cloud
3. taste
4. spot
5. tooth
6. home
7. end
8. pain
9. luck

C Write a sentence that describes what these people do. (Use your dictionary.)

1. An archaeologist
2. A philatelist
3. A physician
4. A producer
5. An editor
6. A cobbler
7. A joiner
8. A farrier
9. An optician
10. A milliner

D Which suffix goes with which meaning? (Use your dictionary.)

1. -able, -ible
2. -ant
3. -on, -oon
4. -ous
5. -ory

A. one who
B. large
C. full of
D. a place for
E. capable of being

33

Reading

 A Read the story.

The Conquest of Space

On the 12th April, 1961, Flight Major Yuri Gagarin became the first person in space when he orbited the Earth in his spacecraft, Vostok I, at a height of 300 kilometres, for an hour and forty- eight minutes. Gagarin became a legend overnight. Quite forgotten now is the tiny female dog named Laika, that four years earlier had the distinction of being the first living creature to orbit Earth and had played a vital role in paving the way for later space flights by humans. In fact, the *quest* to conquer space had started as far back as 1949, when the Russians and Americans earnestly began to grapple with the problems involved. The problems they faced were daunting. It was simply not possible to use aircraft or balloons to *venture* into space because these relied on air to support them, and space was a vacuum, without air. Also, in order to escape from the massive downward pull of the Earth due to *gravity*, it was obvious that what was needed was a totally new vehicle of great power and speed.

To overcome these problems, scientists turned to a thousand-year-old Chinese invention, the rocket. Rockets work in much the same way as any ordinary balloon. When its air is allowed to rush out, it shoots forward. Rockets must burn fuel extremely quickly, so that enough hot gases can be released to shoot the rocket forward into the atmosphere. Unless a rocket can reach – within minutes of lift-off – a speed greater than 29 000 kilometres per hour, it will not escape from the Earth's pull. This speed is called the Earth's escape *velocity*.

Once "escape" from the Earth has been achieved, only very small rocket-power is needed to orbit in space. It takes a spacecraft such as the space shuttle only 90 minutes to orbit Earth. During this time, the astronauts will spend 45 minutes in bright daylight on one side of the Earth and 45 minutes in darkness on the other.

Activities

A **Answer these questions. (Answer in sentence form where possible.)**

1. Who was Yuri Gagarin?
2. What distinction in space history is owed to a dog?
3. What two countries were involved in the "space race"?
4. Why is it so difficult to go from Earth to outer space?
5. Explain how a rocket works.
6. Who invented the rocket?
7. What does the term "escape velocity" mean?
8. How long does it take a space shuttle to orbit the Earth?
9. Write the names of the eight planets in our solar system, and any constellations of stars you know.
10. Find out the meaning of: orbit; distinction; vacuum; grapple; earnest; daunting.
11. Write each of the above words in a sentence of your own.

B **Look up the words in *italics* in your dictionary. Write an interesting sentence for each one.**

C **Summarise the story in your own words. Use about 10 sentences.**

D
"There" or "Their".
(i) **There** means 'in that place'. *The men went there.*
(ii) **There** is used with the verb "to be". *There is (was) a book on the table.*
(iii) **Their** means 'belonging to them', and is always followed by a noun. *I lost their books.*

Write there or their.

1. The swallows built _____ nests _____ last year.
2. _____ feathers are scattered here and _____.
3. I stood _____ watching the birds building _____ nests.
4. _____ was no trace of _____ canary.
5. _____ is an owl in _____ barn.
6. The birds perched _____ with _____ friends the crows.
7. _____ are no eggs _____ yet.
8. _____ and then the hunter shot _____ tame pigeon.
9. Over _____ is a wild animal.
10. Despite _____ efforts _____ pet parrot escaped.

Note: "They're" means "they are".

35

Proofreading

 Find the deliberate mistakes.

Santa Claus was namd after a man who lived on the sothern shor of Turkey. He was a nobleman named Nicholas, and was famus for his generosity. he died about 342 CE. He bekame the patren saint of russia, and of sailors, merchents, children and poeple in sudden danger. we associate him rather with Christmas eve then December 6th which is his feast day.

One Day while out walking Saint Nicholas past an open window. He could here a man and his three daughters bewailing the fact they were pur. All there money was gone. "We will have to beg for moniy to buy food," the distressed father told his daughters.

furthermore the poor man could not afford to give a dowry to aney of his three daughters. In those days a girl without a dowry had littel chance of getting married.

Nicholas was saddined by the plight of the man and his daughters. He had at his home tree bags of gold and He decided to return at night and place one of them inside the window of the poor man's house. This he did when it was dark and the man and his Daughters were asleep.

The next morning the father couldn't believe his eyes. he thanked God for being so merciful towards them. With all this gold the eldest daughter was abel to marry.

On the following night, Nicholas returned with a secund bag of gold. The father was so greatful that he lay awake on the third night saying prayers of thanksgiving to God for been so kind to him in his hour of need. Suddenly he heard a noise. He saw Nicholas place a third bag of gold in his small room. The man ran to Nicholas and fell at his Feet.

"Give thanks to God, for it was he who sent me to you," Nicholas told him.

Nicholas latir became a bishop, and a church was built for him, called the Church of saint Nicholas, in the turkish town of Demre.

36

Grammar

Adjectives

> A sentence can be made more interesting by adding adjectives.
> Example: The boy drank the water.
> The **thirsty** boy drank the **cool** water.

A Write these sentences adding some adjectives.

1. The girl was wearing a green dress.
2. The donkey was in the field.
3. The boy was sitting in the classroom.
4. The detective questioned the man.
5. He stopped the car in a narrow lane.
6. They landed the spaceship on the planet.
7. I saw a clown in his costume.
8. She wrote a letter and left it on the table.
9. The horse was in the forest.
10. The liner crossed the calm ocean.

B Write the missing adjectives.

victorious   expensive   deep   powerful   courageous   famous
graceful   beautiful   friendly   mysterious

1. The gentleman wore a _____ shirt.
2. The _____ policeman rescued the little child.
3. He bought an _____ suit of clothes.
4. He was a _____ swimmer.
5. President Kennedy was a _____ man.
6. The _____ dog wagged his tail.
7. The _____ swan glided through the water.
8. The _____ team was given a great welcome by the enthusiastic crowd.
9. A _____ man appeared at her window.
10. The teenager was drowned in the _____ pool.

C Write six adjectives for each of the following nouns.

1. mountain: rocky; snowy; dangerous; high; bare; misty.
2. dog: _____
3. stream: _____
4. lorry: _____
5. apple: _____
6. doctor: _____
7. lady: _____
8. castle: _____
9. book: _____
10. boat: _____

Writing

How to Write a Letter

(1) Crossways,
6 Hazel Road,
North Shore,
Auckland.

(2) 21/7/2012

(3) Dear Nathan,

(4) I am enjoying my stay here with my cousins in Auckland. Since I arrived, the weather has been sunny, and my cousins have been showing me some of the interesting places in the city. Yesterday we visited the Sky Tower, and earlier today we went to the Zoo. If it stays fine, we will probably go swimming tomorrow.

(5) Your good friend,

(6) Joel.

Every letter must have the six features indicated in the above letter.

(1) The writer's full **address** must be shown at the top right-hand side of the page. The residence, street and postal town must be included in the address. Names of houses begin with capital letters but no quotation marks ("…") are required.
  Examples: Avondale, Beach Grove, Pine Wood, Meadow Court.

(2) The **date** must be clearly indicated. You may write the date in a variety of ways. Here are a few common ways.
  Examples: 3/2/2012   3/2/12   3/2/12   3 February 2012

(3) The **greeting**. Note the use of capital letters and the placing of a comma at the end of the greeting.
  Examples: Dear Mum, Dear Dad and Mum, Dear Mary, Dear Ms Smith, Dear Sir, Dear Madam.

(4) The **message** or content of the letter.

(5) The **ending**. Again, note the use of the capital letter and the placing of the comma.
  Examples: Your loving daughter,   Yours sincerely,
           Your fond son,   Yours truly,
           Your good friend,   Yours respectfully,

(6) The **signature**.

A **Imagine you are staying with friends or relatives who live in another town, city or country. Write a letter to your family or a friend, describing your visit.**

Language

Homonyms

> Homonyms are words having the same sound but with different meanings. They may or may not have the same spelling.
> Example: She sent **two** letters **to** her friend.

A Write these sentences, using the correct homonym.

1. She broke a _____ (*pain, pane*) of glass.
2. There is a hole in the _____ (*sole, soul*) of my shoe.
3. Have a _____ (*piece, peace*) of cake.
4. We had _____ (*serial, cereal*) for breakfast.
5. A basement can be called a _____ (*seller, cellar*).
6. We use a _____ (*plum, plumb*) line to check that a line is vertical.
7. I live in a house with three _____ (*stories, storeys*).
8. Electrical _____ (*currents, currants*) can be dangerous.
9. _____ (*time, thyme*) is a herb.
10. We visited the new golf _____ (*coarse, course*).

B Write these sentences, using the correct homonym.

1. The wind _____ away her _____ hat.
2. He _____ the ball right _____ the window.
3. I _____ the lowing of the _____ in the field.
4. The huge _____ disappeared behind the _____ rock.
5. The girl was so feeble and _____ that she could not attend the concert last _____.
6. She cut her hand on the _____ of glass and it caused her great _____.
7. The boy injured his _____ and it took a long time to _____.
8. The young girl began to _____ when the big _____ struck her on the nose.
9. _____ are books on _____ desks.
10. He _____ his new bicycle on the dusty _____.

blue, blew
threw, through
herd, heard
bare, bear
week, weak
pane, pain
heal, heel
ball, bawl
there, their
road, rode

C Write what each homonym means. Use your dictionary if you wish.

1. Vale / Veil
2. Stile / Style
3. Profit / Prophet
4. Bow / Bough
5. Dew / Due
6. Feet / Feat
7. Foul / Fowl
8. Hale / Hail
9. Key / Quay
10. Leek / Leak
11. Vain / Vein
12. Our / Hour

39

Reading

A Read the story.

The Magnificent Cave

Jim White stopped his horse in amazement. There straight ahead of him over the hills of New Mexico was the most fantastic sight he had ever seen! His eagle eyes told him that the dark buzzing cloud rising from the earth was nothing other than a great mass of whirling bats. Where could they be coming from? Stooping low, the *astonished* cowboy made his way across the rocky ground, where he suddenly came upon a huge hole. What could be down there? Returning the next day, he began to climb down deep into the hole. Soon he saw tunnels on either side of him; so he chose one, lit his lantern and entered. The total silence inside was eerie. When Jim shouted, the echo that returned was so powerful it almost knocked him off his feet! A few steps further and all was explained: Jim White found himself standing in a cave wide enough to hold ten football pitches and high enough for a skyscraper. Hanging from the ceiling were huge icicles of stone. Great pillars, the size of trees, rose from the floor. Jim White was held *spellbound* by the marvellous sculptures of stone his eyes fell upon. This lucky man had discovered the Carlsbad Cavern, the largest, most unique and *spectacular* cave in the world.

On returning to the Triple X ranch that night, he wondered how such a *vast* cavern could have been formed. It had all begun some sixty million years earlier when water seeped through cracks on the surface and started to eat away at the solid rock underneath. The rock in this part of New Mexico was limestone, a soft rock, which is easily worn away by rainwater. Where the rock is particularly soft, huge rooms will be cut out; where the rock is fairly hard, narrow passages will be formed. Jim returned again and again to explore rooms and passageways extending for miles under the New Mexico hills. Today, tourists can *retrace* his footsteps through the magnificent cave, not with the aid of rope and lantern as he once did, but with lifts and electric lights. Each visitor who enters is as enthralled as Jim White was, on that day in June 1901, when he first discovered the Carlsbad Cavern.

Activities

A Answer these questions. (Answer in sentence form where possible.)

1. Where did Jim White live?
2. What did he see rising from the ground one day?
3. Where did the bats come from?
4. Describe the cave he found.
5. How long does it take for such a cave to form?
6. Why did this cave form in this particular part of New Mexico?
7. How has tourism changed the cave?
8. Locate the position of New Mexico, U.S.A., on a map.
9. Write a list of eight words to describe how Jim White felt on first entering the Carlsbad Cavern.
10. Find out the meaning of: whirling; eerie; unique; seeped; extend; enthralled.
11. Write each of the above words in a sentence of your own.

B Look up the words in *italics* in your dictionary. Write an interesting sentence for each one.

C Summarise the story in your own words. Use about 10 sentences.

D Write the correct group term.
Example: a **cluster** of stars.

1. a _____ of stars
2. a _____ of flowers
3. a _____ of eggs
4. a _____ of grapes
5. a _____ of clothes
6. a _____ of furniture
7. a _____ of ships
8. an _____ of soldiers
9. a _____ of players
10. a _____ of dancers
11. a _____ of sailors
12. a _____ of singers
13. a _____ of musicians
14. a _____ of friends

clutch   suite
fleet   group
army   troupe
team   band
crew   choir
bouquet
suit
cluster
bunch

Cloze

A Write the missing words.

river   European   sight   highest   discovering   crash   located
adventurer   knew   thunder   famous   named

Angel Falls

In 1937 when American pilot and _____ Jimmy Angel landed his plane on top of a mountain and got bogged down in a marsh, he didn't find the gold he was looking for. Instead, he found the world's _____ waterfall.

Angel Falls, the highest waterfall in the world, is _____ in the Canaima National Park in Venezuela, South America. The falls are a truly spectacular _____. The water plunges off the edge of a towering table-top mountain, called Auyan Tepui, and falls for 979 metres, 870 metres of which is an uninterrupted drop. The roar of the water as it hits the rocks below is like _____, and there is a constant wall of spray thrown up which veils the _____ valley.

Although Jimmy Angel is widely credited for _____ the falls, the local people, the Pemones, already _____ about the falls, and called them 'Kerepakupai merú', which means "fall from the deepest place". Jimmy Angel wasn't even the first _____ to see the falls. That honour goes to Ernesto de Sánchez La Cruz, who documented finding the falls in 1910. The falls were _____ after Jimmy Angel because he was more _____ than Sánchez La Cruz, and he also had the misfortune to die in a plane _____ near the falls at a later date.

42

Verbs

Grammar

> **Verbs are being or doing words.**
> Example: It **was** cloudy so we **stayed** inside.

A Write the correct verb.

1. The patient _____ (*ran, jumped, hobbled*) around the hospital ward.
2. The post woman _____ (*swam, crept, plodded*) wearily through the snow.
3. The firefighter saw the fire and _____ (*strolled, walked, dashed*) down the street.
4. The baker _____ (*jumped, ran, trotted*) over the low fence.
5. The soldier _____ (*flew, galloped, marched*) across the barrack square.
6. The baby _____ (*sprinted, toddled, strode*) across the floor.
7. The athlete _____ (*staggered, hurried, sprinted*) along the road.
8. The thief _____ (*jumped, dived, prowled*) around the house.

B Write the correct verbs.

hissed	agreed	shrugged	slouched	scrambled	scampered
blared	creaked	leaped	raced	patted	argued	deafened
ground	whirred	attacked	shuffled	mumbled	dragged	shrieked

1. When the door of the old house _____ shut, I _____ outside.
2. The man _____ his dog and it _____ across the park.
3. The snake _____ at the mongoose and then _____ with ferocity.
4. The fugitive's mind _____ as he _____ his feet through the mud.
5. At first we _____ about our favourite film but then we _____.
6. The guilty boy _____ his feet and _____ his shoulders.
7. Our car _____ on for a while, then _____ to a halt.
8. The music _____ so loudly that it _____ the adults.
9. My sister _____ when she saw the mouse and _____ onto a chair.
10. I _____ my apologies to the teacher and _____ into my seat.

C Finish the sentences and underline the verbs.

1. The bee landed on _____
2. The butterfly fluttered near _____
3. The frog swam towards _____
4. The trout darted across _____
5. The squirrel leaped through _____
6. The ant crawled along _____
7. The worm wriggled under _____
8. The rabbit scurried into _____
9. The lambs frisked and frolicked in _____
10. The spider ran into _____

Visits

Writing

In these essays avoid the use of the word "Then". The following words can be used to begin sentences.

> first   soon afterwards   next   almost immediately   shortly afterwards
> presently   no sooner had...than   later on   at the interval
> in the meantime   finally

A   Write about a visit to the dentist. These words and phrases might help you to write the story.

> throbbing toothache
> cheeks puffed and swollen
> waiting anxiously   receptionist
> spotless white coat   big comfortable chair
> gleaming overhead mirror
> mouth inspected   probed and prodded
> needle   pierced   anaesthetic
> gums as cold as ice   forceps
> extraction   decayed tooth   sigh of relief

B   Write about a visit to the circus. These words and phrases might help you to write the story.

> ringmaster's arrival   performing ponies
> trotted, bowed, pranced   brave lion-tamer
> breathtaking act   deathly silence   loud
> applause   comical clowns   funny antics
> daring trapeze artists   somersaulted
> thundered around the arena
> tightrope walker   feats of strength
> magician   performing dogs
> bicycle and balancing pole

44

Language

Homes and Houses

A Homes
State where the following people live and complete each sentence.

1. The queen lives in a _____ in _____ .
2. A hermit lives in a _____ surrounded by _____ .
3. A shepherd lives in a _____ near _____ .
4. A gypsy lives in a _____ beside _____ .
5. A soldier lives in _____ beyond _____ .
6. A convict lives in a _____ during _____ .
7. A lumberjack lives in a _____ in the _____ .
8. An Inuit lives in an _____ in the _____ .

B My house
Fill in the blank spaces with suitable words.

My house is situated _____ . It is a _____ building. Though it is old, it is _____ . There are _____ in it. The bathroom is _____ and painted _____ . The sitting room is very spacious and it has _____ windows. We do our cooking in _____ . In the front of the house there is a lovely _____ with two flower _____ . My mother and I take care of _____ in the garden. The big garden at _____ is cared for by _____ . He grows _____ and _____ . He enjoys _____ there. I love my _____ very much. It is _____ to me than all the world. There is no place like _____ .

C
Compile interesting newspaper advertisements for the following items which you are prepared to rent or sell.

(i) Camping-tent for hire.
(ii) A summer chalet to let.
(iii) A bicycle to sell.
(iv) A guitar or radio to sell.

House for Sale
London
Semi-detached house in beautiful condition, with oil-fired central heating, garage attached, gardens front and rear.

Jones and Smith
Auctioneers
Tel. 369151

45

Reading

A Read the story.

Nanuk

You may meet the Polar Bear at any time and almost anywhere – usually when you least expect him. He may be sitting at your door, or trundle across your trail when you are hunting. You may meet him along the coast, where you have gone to visit your trap lines, or even a hundred kilometres out in the ocean – Mr Polar Bear, calmly riding on a floating iceberg or swimming in the freezing water without effort.

The first time you see him you are shocked. An enormous fat weasel! Such is your impression of his short legs, long body, endless neck and slender snout. He weighs as much as 1000 kilograms, and consequently does not look active, but seems to thunder along slow and unhurried, as clumsy as can be. Do not be deceived; he is just as *agile* in attack as in flight, and in battle is a dangerous enemy. He can gallop when he has to, but his best gait is a trotting stride, wobbly but steady, which he can *maintain* all day long, provided he has not had too much to eat. Food is his weakness.

For the pleasure of *gorging* himself, Nanuk the Bear will take any kind of risk. He will walk right into a camp full of dogs and men, and even into a shack. In really lean days, he will filch seal right off a sledge, though ordinarily he is not a thief. He is an experienced seal-hunter himself. Seal is the only food he really likes, and what he wishes for is the blubber. He cares little for meat, except when he is on his last legs. He loves to play, and if he finds a seal oil drum he is delighted, rolling it downhill, pushing it like a wagon, trundling it like a barrow and finally smashing it to bits, as a child will break a toy he tires of.

In winter, Nanuk will confidently go after a seal under two metres of ice. His *technique* is flawless. He finds the seal's breathing holes in the ice – five or six of them. He selects one and carefully digs into the ice around it. Then he covers the thin ice with snow. Then he sits down, motionless as a marble statue, his left paw poised ready to strike. He will stay at his post, as still as a rock, until the seal comes up to breathe. The bear is so intent on his task that it is quite easy to surprise and kill him while he waits. Sometimes the Inuit hunter waits until he gets the seal first. As soon as the seal comes to the hole, Nanuk's paw comes down. He never misses.

Activities

A **Answer these questions. (Answer them in sentence form where possible.)**

1. To what part of the world does the writer refer?
2. How does the writer show the strength and endurance of the bear?
3. Why might a person not used to polar bears be deceived into thinking the animal is slow and inactive?
4. What might make the bear unable to trot all day long?
5. In what way does the bear resemble a child?
6. How is it shown that Nanuk is a patient and clever animal?
7. "Sometimes, the Inuit hunter waits until he gets the seal first." What advantage do you think the hunter gets by waiting?
8. Give the meaning of: iceberg; lumber along; filch; flawless; confidently.
9. Write each of the above words in a sentence of your own.

B **Look up the words in *italics* in your dictionary. Write an interesting sentence for each one.**

C **Summarise the story in your own words. Use about 10 sentences.**

D "Learn" or "Teach"
To learn means to acquire knowledge or skill by study, practice or teaching.
To teach means to instruct or give knowledge.

Write teach or learn.

1. Let her _____ you how to swim.
2. If you _____ the topics, you will pass the examination.
3. We _____ the same topics as the girls.
4. If I _____ to cycle, I will _____ you during the holidays.
5. Try to _____ quickly. Then you will be able to _____ your brother as he is very slow to _____.
6. The captain likes to _____ the junior boys how to _____ to ride properly.
7. He likes to _____ the girls to _____ to dance gracefully.
8. She will _____ to play the guitar if you _____ her slowly.

47

Fun with Words

A In each of these lists only one word is spelt correctly. Underline the correctly spelt word and correct the other two.

1. countreys, eagle, tabel
2. confuson, Ameirca, deft
3. do'nt, correctley, outer
4. mashine, helicopter, referance
5. peices, kilometres, killograms
6. heavey, quickley, quality
7. definition, queu, flaver
8. capitel, northernly, popular
9. doesn't, oxygin, Febuary
10. preasants, climber, thousands

B How many musical instruments can you find in the wordsearch? There are 12. They can read in any direction. Challenge a friend!

o	n	a	i	p	l	a	b	b	c	c	d
a	a	b	c	y	p	r	a	t	i	u	g
t	d	c	r	p	i	c	c	o	l	o	d
e	l	e	c	l	p	e	l	d	d	i	f
n	e	o	b	o	e	a	u	a	p	p	e
i	c	d	l	o	r	p	b	a	n	j	o
r	c	t	l	r	o	d	e	f	g	u	f
a	p	l	p	g	n	r	i	u	t	p	t
l	e	r	h	a	a	u	b	o	n	j	o
c	c	p	a	n	i	m	f	d	n	t	p
l	h	l	r	h	p	e	t	u	l	f	g
e	m	s	h	k	e	l	g	r	e	o	n

C The following words are common English abbreviations. Write them in full.

1. exam
2. ref
3. photo
4. telly
5. flu
6. sub
7. gym
8. specs

Grammar

Tenses

A **Rewrite these sentences so they are about the future.**

1. I saw him yesterday.
2. The last time I met her, she was very busy.
3. We gathered the sheep and went to the fair.
4. We brought his son to the park on Sunday.
5. I came, I saw, I conquered.
6. I caught a salmon in the river last month.
7. His plan went wrong.
8. The crocodile's teeth glinted in the moonlight.
9. We agreed to meet at the crossroads.
10. The bird flew in a wide circle over the swamp.

B **Write the sentences in the past tense.**

1. I think I see the postman coming down the road.
2. I buy stamps in the Post Office when I go there.
3. I write often to my friend who lives in Abu Dhabi.
4. I collect and deliver the mail.
5. My father drives the train because that is his job.
6. I swim in the lake when the weather is fine.
7. I help my mother when I am on holiday.
8. The old sailor rings the bell and blows the horn whenever there is fog.
9. Every time I hear a knock I expect to see the postman at the door.
10. The man works as a clerk and sells stamps to the customers.

C **Write the verbs in the present tense.**

1. Each of the dolls _____ (to have) a red nose.
2. Neither of the monkeys _____ (to go) into the cage.
3. One of the acrobats _____ (to be) injured.
4. Every man _____ (to know) what to do.
5. Nobody _____ (to wish) to see the man fall.
6. Every one of us _____ (to like) to go to the circus.
7. Not one of the girls _____ (to have) a ticket.
8. Each of the dogs _____ (to be) sick.
9. Each child _____ (to receive) a present.
10. Everybody _____ (to be) delighted with the child's progress.

Writing

Adventures

A While on a camping trip, you found this map in an old ruin. Write about your adventure in search of the treasure.

50

Language

Participles

> Note: The past participle requires another verb with it, the verb "to be" or "to have".
> Examples: (a) He **has** gone. (b) She **was** kept busy. (c) We **were** awakened.

A Write a sentence for each form of the verb – present, past and past participle.

	Present	Past	Past Participle
1.	wake	woke	woken
2.	rise	rose	risen
3.	beat	beat	beaten
4.	blow	blew	blown
5.	begin	began	begun
6.	choose	chose	chosen
7.	bite	bit	bitten
8.	come	came	come
9.	fly	flew	flown
10.	know	knew	known

B Write these sentences, using the correct form of the verb.

1. He has just (wrote, written) to his cousin to ask him if he had (took, taken) the book.
2. After he had (sung, sang) the song, I (spoke, speak) to him.
3. If I had (rang, rung) the bell she would have (woke, woken) in time.
4. Before I (ate, eaten) my dinner I went and (swam, swum) in the lake.
5. The coat which he (worn, wore) had been (stole, stolen).
6. He had (took, taken) the day off because he (is, was) sick.
7. The gardener (stood, stand) near the hole he had (dug, dig).
8. The whistle was (blown, blew) and the game (began, begun).
9. The mother cried because she (known, knew) that her son had done the robbery.
10. When he had (drew, drawn) the picture he (gave, give) it to the lady.

C Fill in the past and past participle form of each verb.

	Present	Past	Past Participle
1.	give	gave	given
2.	go	_____	_____
3.	hold	_____	_____
4.	know	_____	_____
5.	ring	_____	_____
6.	rise	_____	_____
7.	sing	_____	_____
8.	speak	_____	_____
9.	stand	_____	_____
10.	steal	_____	_____

Reading

A Read the text.

The Titanic

Containing 11 decks and stretching a full 305 metres, she was the greatest ocean liner of her time. The ship had been fitted out in true style, with plush cabins, electric lifts, squash courts, gymnasium and a heated indoor swimming pool. There was a hospital to cope with any passengers who became ill; and to cater for meals, she carried a dinner service of 100,000 plates. The owners, the shipbuilders, the captain – in fact everyone – said the Titanic was unsinkable. Perhaps this was the reason why only enough lifeboats for half of the passengers were placed on board. Tickets for her *maiden voyage* were snapped up eagerly, and there were over 2,000 people on board when she set out from Southampton for New York on April 11th, 1912.

Disaster was to strike after only four days at sea. With a captain and crew determined to break the record for an Atlantic crossing, the liner had been ploughing through calm, glass-like seas at a speed of 22 knots. She had entered an area known as the Grand Banks when two radio reports from other ships were received, warning of icebergs. The warnings were ignored. The Titanic steamed ahead at full speed. It was almost midnight when Frederick Fleet, the look-out in the crow's nest, suddenly spotted an iceberg looming ahead in the darkness. But his frantic warning cries were too late to prevent *collision*. A huge hole was ripped into the side of the liner and the water poured in.

At first, the passengers treated the incident as a joke; yet, within ten minutes, the water had risen five metres inside the ship. Distress signals were sent out to the nearby liner, the California, but her radio had unfortunately been switched off. Panic now spread, as the huge liner listed to one side and began to sink. By the time another liner, the Carpathia, finally arrived to help, 1,500 people had drowned in the icy seas. The loss of the Titanic was one of the greatest *catastrophes* in the history of navigation.

Activities

A **Answer these questions. (Answer in sentence form where possible.)**

1. What major safety error did the builders of the Titanic make?
2. Why was such a basic error allowed to occur?
3. Describe the Titanic.
4. What was the destination of her maiden voyage?
5. What blunder did the captain make?
6. Why did Frederick Fleet become alarmed?
7. Why did the California not come to help the stricken liner?
8. How many people drowned?
9. Pretend you are a newspaper reporter in 1912. Write a paragraph about the loss of the Titanic.
10. Find out the meaning of: plush; frantic; looming; incident; listed.
11. Write each of the above words in a sentence of your own.

B **Look up the words in *italics* in your dictionary. Write an interesting sentence for each one.**

C **Summarise the story in your own words. Use about 10 sentences.**

D **Write the phrases with the correct word.**

| trickle pot spread flake beam crumb pinch puff grain |
| ray breath morsel |

1. a _____ of salt
2. a _____ of sand
3. a _____ of tea
4. a _____ of water
5. a _____ of butter
6. a _____ of bread
7. a _____ of food
8. a _____ of sunshine
9. a _____ of light
10. a _____ of wind
11. a _____ of air
12. a _____ of snow

Cloze

A Write the missing words.

~~brings~~   into   ~~old~~   ~~Eve~~   visitor   doubly   ~~called~~   ~~good~~

In Scotland, New Year's _____ is _____ Hogmanay! An _____ custom welcomes _____ each house a dark-haired man, called a "first-footer", and this _____ is thought to bring _____ luck. He usually _____ gifts to the family, which makes him _____ welcome!

B Write the missing words.

performed   ~~most~~   ~~wheelbarrow~~   ~~back~~   ~~on~~   across   ~~walked~~   Frenchman   ~~carried~~

Charles Blondin was a _____, born in 1824. He was a tightrope walker, and he _____ his dangerous feats in _____ unusual places. On one occasion, he _____ a tight rope blindfolded, pushing a _____, and another time he _____ a man on his _____ as he walked _____ Niagara Falls _____ a tightrope.

C Write the missing words.

Bats are not blind, although _____ may say "as _____ as a bat!" You see, these little mammals do not _____ entirely on _____ eyes. Their ears are more important! A bat _____ as it flies, and the sound bounces _____ from any nearby object. The bat's _____ ears pick up the _____, and it swerves to _____ the obstacle. The bat's squeak is _____ high for our ears, but special machines can _____ it up.

54

Grammar

Adverbs

> **Adverbs are words which tell us more about verbs. Most adverbs are made by adding -ly to adjectives or -ily if the adjective already ends in -y.**

A **Write this passage and underline the adverbs.**

He ran quickly down the street. He looked anxiously left and right. Fortunately everything was quiet. He felt tired and rather unhappy to be running away so soon. He reached the crossroads and stopped. He started again and turned into the High Street. Suddenly he stopped. There was the sound of footsteps behind him. His heart beat violently. He was being followed!

B **Write a suitable adverb and complete each sentence.**

1. The prince spoke _____ to _____.
2. The robber left _____ when _____.
3. The goalkeeper _____ caught the ball and _____.
4. We worked _____ until _____.
5. The swallow flew _____ through _____.
6. Pancho's father shouted _____ when _____.
7. The postman walked _____ along _____.
8. Shin wept _____ because _____.
9. The soldiers fought _____ but _____.
10. The river flowed _____ towards _____.

C **Change the following adjectives into adverbs. Write a sentence for each.**

1. calm   calmly
2. warm   _____
3. bitter   _____
4. fresh   _____
5. final   _____
6. reckless   _____
7. sweet   _____
8. coward   _____
9. happy   _____
10. equal   _____
11. noisy   _____
12. scarce   _____
13. brave   _____
14. cruel   _____
15. loud   _____
16. foolish   _____
17. rapid   _____
18. patient   _____
19. wise   _____
20. heavy   _____

Writing

Suitable Endings

A Write a suitable ending to the following story.

Paul saw a large-looking creature bury itself in the sand and slowly crawl under the rock. Cautiously he groped about in the sand with his fingers. Suddenly . . .

> A useful vocabulary of phrases:
> sharp claws   clung to his fingers   pinched   screamed with pain   shook
> the crab   trickle of blood   crab crawled slowly away

B Write a suitable ending to this story.

On a beautiful June day, I mounted my bicycle and headed into the countryside. My destination was a lovely valley nestling among the hills.
   At last, hot and panting, I arrived at my destination. I dismounted slowly . . .

> A useful vocabulary of phrases:
> the tall pines   a rocky hill   humming of birds   murmuring stream
> chirping of birds   sparkling lake   winding river   sighing of the wind
> rustling of the leaves   majestic waterfall

C Write a suitable ending to the story.

It was a beautiful May morning. Farmer Daly went out early to the field to count the young lambs. Just as he was about to enter the field, he spied a huge eagle soaring in the sky. Suddenly . . .

56

Language

Quotation Marks

> Only the spoken words are written inside the quotation marks.
> Examples: "I think those dark clouds are a sign of rain," said Lantz.
> Mary says, "He is a fantastic pop singer."
> "Who is the camp leader?" asked Yasmin.

"I think those dark clouds are a sign of rain."

"He is a fantastic pop singer!"

"Who is the camp leader?"

A   **Write quotation marks, capital letters, exclamation marks, commas and question marks where needed.**

1. The conductor announced The bus is full.
2. Helen said I dislike going to the dentist.
3. The farmer shouted Close the gate after you.
4. Femi whispered It is hidden underneath the stone.
5. The doctor asked Did you ever have the measles?
6. Ann enquired Where is the new museum?
7. Abid asked When are we getting our holidays?
8. You have broken my new pen sobbed Mark.
9. I am the best footballer boasted Hari.
10. When did you arrive enquired her mother.
11. May I borrow your English book requested Fu.
12. Who scored the last goal asked Ruth.
13. Have you any old shoes asked the beggar.
14. The inspector asked Who can recite the poem.
15. Mrs Singh remarked My daughter has passed the examination.
16. Tom shouted Don't go without me.

Reading

A Read the funny stories.

The Burglar Who Called the Police

✻ The Least Successful Weather Report ✻

After severe flooding in Jeddah in January 1979, the Arab News gave the following bulletin: "We regret we are unable to give you the weather. We rely on weather reports from the airport, which is closed because of the weather. Whether we are able to give you the weather tomorrow depends on the weather."

✻ The Funeral That Disturbed a Corpse ✻

Perhaps the most unsuccessful funeral service ever held was that of an *oriental* missionary called Schwartz. The service was held in Delhi at the end of the nineteenth century and *culminated* in the congregation singing the favourite hymn of the recently deceased Dr Schwartz. The mourners were surprised during the final verse to hear a voice from the coffin joining in.

✻ The "Perfect Crime" ✻

A New York burglar committed what many regard as the perfect crime in 1969. Following a carefully prepared plan, he climbed up on the roof of a supermarket which he intended to burgle. Once there he discovered that he could not enter the building since the skylight was *marginally* too small to slip through. With a sudden flash of *inspiration* he removed all his clothes and dropped them in through the skylight intending to follow them seconds later. However, he was still unable to fit through and had to call the police to get his clothes back.

"You will never amount to very much" – a Munich schoolmaster to Albert Einstein, aged 10.

58

Activities

A **Answer these questions. (Answer in sentence form where possible.)**

1. Where was the funeral service held?
2. Why were the mourners surprised?
3. What did the schoolmaster say to Albert Einstein?
4. Why are these words ironic?
5. What building was the burglar standing on?
6. Why did the burglar remove his clothes?
7. How did he get his clothes back?
8. Why was the Arab News unable to give the weather?
9. Why was the airport closed?
10. Which of the four funny facts was your favourite?

B **Look up the words in *italics* in your dictionary.
Write an interesting sentence for each one.**

C **'Lot' is an overused word.
Rewrite the sentences using another word.**

> much   all   crowd   selection   many   plenty
> spectators   variety   troupe   abundance

1. After the game **a lot of people** invaded the football pitch.
2. The fisherman had an **awful lot** of fresh herring for sale.
3. **A lot** people dislike spiders.
4. I bought a **whole lot** of the records.
5. The robbers stole **a lot** of the money.
6. There is an **awful lot** of wheat grown in Canada.
7. **Lots of** reasons were given for his poor performance.
8. The audience was entertained by a **lot** of Spanish dancers.
9. A **lot** of people in the street watched the fire.
10. **A lot of** the boys in my class are going to the game.

D **Write the phrases.**

> means   there   easy   go   out   ends   all   far   about   square
> again   forth   parcel   thin   sound

1. Odds and _____
2. Near and _____
3. Out and _____
4. One and _____
5. Down and _____
6. Ways and _____
7. Back and _____
8. Here and _____
9. Fair and _____
10. Time and _____
11. Free and _____
12. Touch and _____
13. Thick and _____
14. Safe and _____
15. Part and _____

Fun with Words

A Only one spelling in each line is correct. Underline the correctly spelt word and correct the other two.

1. paralell, waltz, librarien
2. chickin, necessary, fourty
3. graceful, dispise, destiney
4. fruitfull, friar, galexy
5. liase, lethel, liquid
6. middel, nonsence, oxygen
7. ostrich, parsly, proffessor
8. ravenos, prettie, creature
9. diferent, emerald, dimond
10. gorila, goblit, parcel

B How many birds can you find in the wordsearch? They can read in any direction. Challenge a friend!

b	m	a	l	i	n	n	e	c	o	o	t
i	m	u	c	r	o	b	i	n	h	e	n
t	a	k	k	r	d	m	d	u	c	k	e
t	g	g	i	o	o	i	e	l	a	r	k
e	p	r	w	w	d	w	a	e	l	s	c
r	i	e	i	l	o	h	g	e	e	s	e
n	e	b	g	u	l	l	l	n	k	e	l
i	r	e	r	a	r	e	e	g	r	o	e
d	s	w	i	f	t	n	h	e	r	o	n
o	r	a	v	e	n	e	w	r	e	n	w
v	e	s	w	a	l	l	o	w	g	g	o
e	l	i	n	n	e	t	u	d	a	n	e

C Write the sentences, using the most suitable word.

1. The _____ (*big, great, tiny*) flea jumped a long way.
2. A _____ (*small, huge, little*) giant of a man stepped into the ring.
3. A _____ (*little, great, enormous*) baby crawled into the caravan.
4. The _____ (*tall, large, little*) giraffe ate all the bananas.
5. The strong man bent a _____ (*large, tiny, small*) iron bar.
6. The _____ (*big, tall, little*) lamb was just born.
7. The ship struck a _____ (*great, small, tiny*) rock and sank.
8. The _____ (*little, big, small*) elephant thundered around the ring.

Grammar

Adjectives and Adverbs

A Find the adjectives and the adverbs.

Yesterday I saw two blackbirds building their nest. They flew backwards and forwards, carrying twigs and dried grass from which they carefully wove a little round basket. They continuously pulled and tugged at it until they were completely satisfied with the shape. Then they lined the nest with a mixture of mud. They cleverly smoothed the inside with their little bodies. When the mud was dry it was as hard as cement. Soon the female blackbird would lay her eggs.

B Write a suitable adjective from the given list, and complete each sentence.

huge   agile   spotted   timid   clumsy   tiny   lean
majestic   cunning   frightened

1. The _____ bear lumbered _____.
2. The _____ leopard sprang _____.
3. The _____ deer bounded _____.
4. The _____ elephant ambled _____.
5. The _____ lion prowled _____.
6. The _____ monkey climbed _____.
7. The _____ wolf loped _____.
8. The _____ rabbit scurried _____.
9. The _____ fox sneaked _____.
10. The _____ mouse scampered _____.

C Find the adjectives and adverbs from the given nouns.

Nouns	Adjectives	Adverbs
1. patience	patient	patiently
2. vacancy	_____	_____
3. silence	_____	_____
4. kindness	_____	_____
5. intelligence	_____	_____
6. skill	_____	_____
7. quietness	_____	_____
8. happiness	_____	_____

Writing

Reviews

A **Film Review:** Choose a film you have seen and answer these questions to help you review it. Draw a favourite scene from the film.

1. Name of film: _____
2. Duration: _____
3. Main actors: _____
4. Main characters: _____
5. Director's name: _____
6. Write a one-sentence summary of the film.
7. Which three of these adjectives best describe the film: brilliant, scary, far-fetched, stupid, uneventful, boring, intriguing, dated?
   _____
8. To what age group is this film best suited?
   _____
9. How many marks (out of 10) would you award this film? _____
10. Would you recommend this film to a friend? Why (not)?
    _____

B **Book Review:** Choose a book and answer these questions to help you write your book review.

1. Name of book: _____
2. Author: _____
3. Number of pages: _____
4. How long did it take you to read?
   _____
5. Main characters: _____
6. Write a one-sentence summary of the book.
7. Which three of these adjectives best describe the book: imaginative, dull, exciting, superb, far-fetched, nail-biting, uneventful, monotonous, intriguing, old-fashioned?
   _____
8. To what age group is this book best suited?
   _____
9. How many marks (out of 10) would you award this book? Why?
   _____
10. Would you read another book by the same author? Why (not)?
    _____

Language

> A simile is the comparison of one thing with another.
> Example: I'm as hungry as a wolf.

A Complete these similes.

lamb   wolf   honey   lark   church mouse   daisy   ice
eel   hills   berry   bee   horse   putty   owl   mule   snow
lightning   new pin   grass   peacock   crystal

1. As fresh as a _____
2. As busy as a _____
3. As poor as a _____
4. As soft as _____
5. As quick as _____
6. As old as the _____
7. As clean as a _____
8. As clear as _____
9. As green as _____
10. As happy as a _____
11. As proud as a _____
12. As white as _____
13. As strong as a _____
14. As gentle as a _____
15. As brown as a _____
16. As hungry as a _____
17. As stubborn as a _____
18. As cold as _____
19. As slippery as an _____
20. As wise as an _____
21. As sweet as _____

B Fill in these analogies.
Example: Author is to book as artist is to picture.

1. Bee is to hive as horse is to _____.
2. _____ is to hearing as eye is to sight.
3. Author is to book as _____ is to picture.
4. Table is to _____ as window is to glass.
5. Beautiful is to ugly as dark is to _____.
6. School is to _____ as _____ is to doctor.
7. Feather is to _____ as _____ is to _____.
8. _____ is to _____ as _____ is to kitten.

C Give the singular of the following words.

1. armies _____
2. feet _____
3. mice _____
4. foxes _____
5. tomatoes _____
6. oxen _____
7. fairies _____
8. roofs _____
9. geese _____
10. thrushes _____
11. loaves _____
12. teeth _____

Reading

A Read the text.

Gold

The discovery of gold in California in the nineteenth century caused an *outbreak* of a strange, new "disease" known as gold fever. People became so gripped by the lure of gold that they actually showed all the symptoms of a fever – sleeplessness, restlessness and hot, nervous excitement. A side effect of this fever was a doubling of the population of California in a short space of time! One of those bitten by the gold bug was a certain E.H. Hargreaves, who travelled all of 6,500 kilometres from Australia in search of Californian gold. Unfortunately, he arrived too late. His journey was not a complete waste of effort, however, for Hargreaves spent the time in California studying the type of rock and landscape most likely to yield gold!

Equipped with this knowledge, he returned to Australia in 1851 and immediately announced to his friends that he was about to take a canoe down the Macquarie River in search of gold. His friends just laughed and said he was mad. Nevertheless, the undaunted Hargreaves set off on his expedition, accompanied by a bushman named Lister. A long, difficult journey finally brought them to a small *creek* along the river, whereupon Hargreaves suddenly had a strange overpowering feeling that there was gold everywhere about them. When he told Lister, the bushman was convinced that Hargreaves had indeed gone stark, raving mad. Then Hargreaves stooped down and dug up a handful of mud . . . it was full of glittering, sparkling gold!

When the discovery was announced in the papers on the 15th May, 1851, it caused an immediate outbreak of gold fever. Thousands upon thousands deserted their jobs and rushed to begin digging all over the countryside. Many were successful. One man dug up 15 kilograms of gold in a single hour; another found a single *nugget* worth £12,000, a huge sum in those days. It was Hargreaves's turn to laugh now – all the way to the bank.

Activities

A Answer these questions. (Answer in sentence form where possible).

1. What effect did gold have on people?
2. What effect did the discovery of gold have on California?
3. How did Hargreaves put his journey to California to good use?
4. Why did his friends think he was mad?
5. Did Hargreaves go alone on his expedition?
6. Give reasons why you think the journey down the Macquarie River was difficult.
7. Write six words to describe how Hargreaves must have felt when he noticed gold in the mud of the river.
8. Imagine you were in Australia when the discovery of gold was first announced. Write a paragraph to describe what you saw.
9. Use a map to locate the position of California in the USA and the Macquarie River in Australia.
10. Find out the meaning of these words: lure; yield; undaunted; symptoms.

B Look up the words in *italics* in your dictionary. Write an interesting sentence for each one.

C Summarise the story in your own words. Use about 10 sentences.

D "Walked" and "Went" are overused words. Write the sentences using other words.

> charged   crept   prowled   strolled   toddled   shuffled   limped   plodded
> staggered   hobbled   dashed   marched   waded   stepped   sauntered

1. The daring fireman _____ quickly _____.
2. The lame man _____ slowly _____.
3. The young boy _____ noisily _____.
4. The brave hunter _____ stealthily _____.
5. The injured player _____ painfully _____.
6. The weary boxer _____ helplessly _____.
7. The old postman _____ wearily _____.
8. The clever burglar _____ silently _____.
9. The courageous soldier _____ bravely _____.
10. The old lady _____ feebly _____.
11. The wise fisherman _____ cautiously _____.
12. The American tourist _____ casually _____.
13. The chubby baby _____ haltingly _____.
14. The happy teenagers _____ slowly _____.
15. The nervous woman _____ hurriedly _____.

65

Cloze

A Write the missing words.

easy cell strait fierce top lock Houdini its which
escape artist unable top fully could unawares dearly manacled
minutes upside his dropped thick York possess stomach time
later unlocking feats minutes

Neither chain, _____ or manacle could ever hold Harry Houdini. Many a convict would _____ have loved to _____ his magical powers, for time after _____ he proved that even _____ security prisons were _____ to hold him. In Washington Jail he was _____ and locked without _____ clothes in Murderer's Row; within five _____ he had his _____ door open and began _____ all the other cells; a few minutes _____ he arrived in the warden's office, _____ dressed. In New _____ they wrapped him in a _____ jacket and hung him _____ down from the _____ of a skyscraper. Houdini escaped easily. But the Delaware River was not so _____: it was covered in _____ ice when the handcuffed Houdini was _____ through a hole into _____ deep, freezing waters. Six terrible _____ passed before _____ struggled to the surface. One of his regular _____ was to show how he _____ take hard punches to the _____ without discomfort. Unfortunately, one night a student caught him _____ with a _____ punch which left him badly injured and from _____ he never recovered. On October 31st 1926, Harry Houdini, the great _____ died.

66

Grammar

The Comma

> The comma indicates a brief pause.
>
> **Rules**
> 1. It is used to indicate the person spoken to.
>   Example: Hello, Vera, may I speak to your brother?
> 2. It is used to show a sequence of actions.
>   Example: I opened the can, emptied the contents and strained the juice.
> 3. It is used when one writes a list of nouns or adjectives, verbs or adverbs in a sentence without employing any conjunctions.
>   Example: I ate a large, red, rosy apple.
> 4. It is used to separate phrases beginning with a present participle (...ing).
>   Example: Jumping over the wall, he injured his back.
> 5. It is used before nouns in apposition (nouns closely related to each other).
>   Example: Paris, the capital of France, is a beautiful city.

A Write these sentences, inserting commas.

1. I saw tigers lions monkeys and elephants at the circus.
2. We bought milk butter tea and sugar.
3. Rome Paris Madrid and London are capital cities.
4. They sold classical modern and folk records.
5. My bedroom is warm cosy and comfortable.
6. Cheerio David until we meet again.
7. The robber snatched the money dashed out the door and escaped.
8. He washed the clothes hung them out to dry and later ironed them.
9. Feeling happy with the result I departed for London.
10. Having dug the garden she planted the seeds.

B Use the above five rules to insert commas in these sentences.

1. "Halah ask John for the new book."
2. "Ladies and Gentlemen the show is about to commence."
3. Margaret yawned closed her eyes and fell asleep.
4. Peter stood up opened the book and began to read.
5. The house was cold damp and empty.
6. The kangaroo jumped leaped hopped and skipped.
7. Having bought a new rod I decided to go fishing.
8. Being the fastest runner she won the race.
9. Mount Everest the highest mountain in the world was conquered by Sir Edmund Hillary and Sherpa Tenzing.
10. Napoleon a famous general was exiled to the island of Elba.

Writing

Things That Make Me Mad

A Make a list of some things that make you mad.
Examples
1. Touchy people!
2. When I trip on my shoelaces!
3. When I get blamed for something my brother did!

1. _____
2. _____
3. _____
4. _____
5. _____
6. _____
7. _____
8. _____
9. _____
10. _____

B Dragons

1. Think of the many uses a dragon's fire breathing could be put to. List them.

2. Design an advertisement for a Knight and Dragon Jousting Tournament.

3. Create your own imaginary dragon.
   What is its name?
   Where does it live?
   What foods are its favourite?
   Describe what it looks like.

Language

A Complete these expressions. Write what they mean.

> eye   milk   bush   end   bag   tears   blanket   leaf   music   bonnet
> water   hatchet   horse   teacup   diamond   cold
> waters   forward   head

1. A storm in a _____
2. To put the cart before the _____
3. To cry over spilt _____
4. At a loose _____
5. A wet _____
6. The apple of one's _____
7. To put one's best foot _____
8. To hit the nail on the _____
9. To turn over a new _____
10. To get into hot _____
11. A rough _____
12. To face the _____
13. To let the cat out of the _____
14. To bury the _____
15. To shed crocodile _____
16. To blow hot and _____
17. To have a bee in one's _____
18. To beat about the _____
19. To pour oil on troubled _____

B Write one word for each group of words in *italics*.
Example: In the garage smoking was **not allowed**.   prohibited

1. The school concert is held *once every year*.   a_____
2. In winter, the frog *goes for a long rest*.   h_____
3. The game was *put off* until next week.   p_____
4. We must leave *at once* if we are to catch the school bus.   i_____
5. Every year the swallows *fly from one country to another*.   m_____
6. *Over and over again* he played the same tune.   r_____
7. The explorer told a story about *people who ate human flesh*.   c_____
8. I consulted the *list of books* in the library.   c_____
9. The flowers were *not real but made of plastic*.   a_____
10. He wrote his *life story*.   a_____

Reading

A Read the text.

Mysteries of Migration

The *migration* of birds was a source of complete mystery to people in *bygone* times. For example, because people never saw the nests, eggs, or chicks of the Barnacle goose, they could not understand how these fully-grown birds magically appeared in Ireland each autumn. The best explanation given – and this was believed by all – was that Barnacle geese simply hatched out of barnacles at the bottom of the sea, and hence the name.

Today, other mysteries of migration are being unravelled. At the end of each summer an estimated 4,000 million birds migrate from Europe to spend the winter in Africa and Asia. Of these, at least half will be dead by the following spring. Nevertheless, there can be no doubt that extremely accurate navigation is involved in these journeys. Even the young cuckoo, abandoned by its parents, will still be able to travel on its own all the way to Africa for winter. The question that puzzled scientists for so long was: how can these birds navigate so well, both by day and by night? It now seems certain that migrating birds use the position of the Sun and stars, as well as their own sense of smell and sound, in finding their way. Even more fascinating is the new discovery that birds also use magnetism to navigate. Bird tissue has been found to contain magnetite, which is the basic mineral in magnets. This magnetite somehow acts on the Earth's magnetic field to give the bird a sense of North-South direction. Proof of this can be seen by strapping a tiny magnet to the wings of a homing pigeon. The magnet will interfere with the bird's own magnetic sense, thus making it very difficult to find its way home. Using these varied methods in navigation, it is possible for the migrating bird to cover enormous distances with pin-point *accuracy*.

Activities

A Answer these questions (Answer in sentence form where possible.)

1. Why was the migration of birds a source of mystery to people in bygone times?
2. How did the Barnacle goose get its name?
3. At what time of the year do 4,000 million birds migrate from Europe, and where do they go?
4. How do migrating birds navigate?
5. What question puzzled scientists for so long?
6. What new discovery has been made about migration?
7. How does magnetite help birds to find their way? Can it be proved?
8. Write a paragraph about birds.
9. Find out the meaning of these words: navigate; unravelled; estimated; interfere.
10. Write each of the above words in a sentence of your own.

B Look up the words in *italics* in your dictionary.
Write an interesting sentence for each one.

C Summarise the text in your own words. Use about 10 sentences.

D Insert the correct phrase for each sentence.

> again and again   above and beyond   spick and span   hand and foot
> hammer and tongs   neck and neck   touch and go   wear and tear
> here and there   odds and ends

1. The basket contained an assortment of _____.
2. Mansa keeps her house _____.
3. The two horses passed the winning post _____.
4. The doctor said that it would be _____ if the patient lived.
5. He tried _____ until he succeeded.
6. The man's clothes were scattered _____ on the rocks.
7. Thomas received extra money for the _____ of his car.
8. She worked _____ to pass her examination.
9. The faithful maid waited _____ on her mistress.
10. The policeman risked his life _____ the call of duty.

Cloze

A Write the missing words.

> opportunity   fascinated   talented   probed   together   whom   families
> followed   awarded   sharing   killed   Swedish   mathematics   elder
> continued   disease   harsh   malignant   received   study   scientists   used
> commemorated   awarded

One of the greatest _____ of all time, Marie Sklodowska Curie, is _____ on stamps.

   The daughter of a schoolmaster, Marie was born in Warsaw in 1867. She was clever, but Poland at that time was under the _____ rule of the Russian Tsars and there was little _____ of higher education for Polish girls, however _____.

Marie was _____ by science and longed to study it. Eventually, by taking posts as a governess with wealthy _____, she was able to help her _____ sister Bronya to go to Paris to _____ medicine. She herself _____ as soon as she had saved sufficient money.

   While studying _____ and physics at the Sorbonne (the University of Paris), Marie met a French scientist, Pierre Curie, _____ she married.

The story of their partnership is well known – how, working _____, they _____ the secrets of radioactivity of metals, and discovered radium, which could be _____ to cure, for the first time in history, certain _____ types of the _____ called cancer.

   For their discoveries, the Curies were _____, in 1903, the Nobel Prize for Physics, _____ it with another French scientist, Henry Bacqueret. Unhappily, Pierre Curie was _____ in a street accident in Paris in 1906, but Marie Curie _____ her work as a scientist, and, in 1911, _____ a second of these great _____ honours when she was _____ the Nobel Prize for Chemistry.

Grammar

The Apostrophe (')

When we want to show that something belongs to someone, we use an apostrophe.

Examples: the boy's trainers = the trainers of the boy
the boys' trainers = the trainers of the boys

Note: (a) If a word ends in s already, just add the apostrophe.
(b) If the plural does not end in s, we add 's.

A Write these sentences, inserting the apostrophes where they are needed.

1. Leannes hat is in the monkeys cage.
2. She took my friends pen from the teachers desk.
3. Mrs Smiths car is parked on Main Street.
4. I found the postmans hat on the road.
5. The pupils magazine was in tatters.
6. The boys fishing hook got caught in Sanjays scarf.
7. I borrowed my neighbours tractor.
8. Zindels trousers were sent for repairs.
9. The boys coat was floating in the pond.

B Write these sentences, using an apostrophe to change the underlined words.

1. The case was packed with clothes for men.
2. The hands of the clock didn't move.
3. The nose of the thief was bleeding.
4. The wife of the presenter sang sweetly.
5. The nests of the birds were beautifully made.
6. The toys of the children were scattered on the floor.
7. I stayed at the farm of my aunt.
8. The chain of the mayor disappeared.

C Its and It's
Its means belonging to something, for example: The dog's coat is silky and its collar is blue.
It's means 'it is' or 'it has' for example: It's a pity it's not a fine day. It's been snowing heavily.

Write it's or its.

1. _____ not clear if _____ back is broken.
2. The soup has lost _____ flavour.
3. The peacock is proud of _____ feathers.
4. The swallow returned to _____ nest.
5. _____ a shame that _____ cover is torn.

Writing

Friendships

Friends don't always agree with each other. Look at the pictures below. Would you agree to do this? Explain why.

A

Your friend asks you to take a short cut across the railway line.

_____
_____
_____

B

Your friend asks if he/she can cut your hair for you.

_____
_____
_____

Language

A Write the answers. The words begin with "A".

1. It is sometimes called "The Fall".
2. When people disagree they sometimes have an _____ .
3. A type of nut.
4. We need it for television reception.
5. The largest of the five continents.
6. The joint connecting foot and leg.
7. It chains a ship to the sea bottom.
8. Worn by a cook.
9. In which month is Fool's Day?
10. There are three in a triangle.
11. They draw and paint.
12. We breathe it.
13. Height above sea level.
14. They are hard-working insects.
15. A person who fishes.
16. She takes part in plays and films.
17. A special day.
18. Branching horn of a deer.
19. A popular fruit.

B Quiz: How many answers can you write?

1. The imaginary line which divides the Earth into two hemispheres. _____
2. A bactrian camel has two humps. A _____ only has one.
3. Mackerel, plaice, cod, trout. Which is the freshwater fish? _____
4. Where do "conkers" come from? _____
5. A female sheep is called a _____ .
6. Is the whale a fish? _____
7. Which is the biggest bird in the world? _____
8. A badger lives in a _____ .
9. How many arms does an octopus have? _____
10. Which animal is called "King of the Beasts"? _____
11. What would you find in an apiary? _____
12. A female fox is called a _____ .

Reading

A Read the story.

The Enchanted Stag
(A tale from North America)

Two Native American children, Wabi and Kato, were *banished* into the forest by their wicked stepmother. Strange faces among the trees frightened them as they walked along hand in hand.

"Look, there is a stag's trail," cried Kato suddenly. "His tracks will lead us out of the forest." They soon came to a spreading oak tree and decided to pitch their wigwam in its shade.

Wabi was thirsty, and seeing water in a large hoofprint, knelt to drink. After one sip, he began to feel funny. Antlers sprouted from his head, a white fur covered his body and he grew hooves.

Wabi had turned into a white deer, and immediately they heard their stepmother's voice. "Nobody will ever be able to save him, unless they fell this oak tree." Kato looked up, but saw nothing.

When Kato tried to knock down the tree, her little *tomahawk* splintered and broke. She lay down and cried herself to sleep against the soft fur of the gentle stag.

Days passed. Each morning, the stag trotted off to graze and remained away until evening. One day, he galloped home at midday, *pursued* by hunters. Among the braves, Kato recognised her father.

Kato told them the whole story. "We will burn down the oak," said one of the hunters. Soon the tree came crashing down, and the stag immediately changed into a boy. Wabi was saved.

Out of the smoke, a black owl flew screeching into the forest. "Our stepmother was a witch," said Wabi softly. "Now, she must *dwell* for ever with the evil spirits of the forest."

Activities

A Answer these questions. (Answer in sentence form where possible.)

1. Who banished the children into the forest?
2. Where did they pitch their wigwam?
3. Where was the puddle of water?
4. What was the stepmother's spell?
5. Why was Kato unable to knock down the tree?
6. At what time of day did Kato recognise her father?
7. What came out of the smoke?
8. The stepmother was actually a _____ .
9. Name another story where the stepmother was wicked.

B Look up the words in *italics* in your dictionary.
Write an interesting sentence for each one.

C Summarise the story in your own words. Use about 10 sentences.

D Write **of** and **off**.

1. The clown ran _____ with one _____ the balloons.
2. Which _____ you switched _____ the light?
3. He galloped _____ ahead _____ the rest _____ them.
4. The rest _____ the girls saw Mary dive _____ the rock.
5. The teacher asked the two _____ us to turn _____ the water.
6. He took _____ his coat because _____ the heat.
7. I set _____ on the journey with the rest _____ the hikers.
8. The aeroplane took _____ at the end _____ the runway.
9. Several _____ the players were ordered _____ the field.
10. The younger _____ the two girls was afraid _____ the monkeys.
11. A bag full _____ flour fell _____ the lorry.

Fun with Words

A In each of these lists only one word is spelt correctly. Underline the correctly spelt word and correct the other two.

1. sentense, phrase, normaly
2. prisonar, needey, parliament
3. emotion, hankerchief, punckual
4. innocense, honnest, famous
5. knoledge, discription, length
6. excellense, defence, desision
7. splendur, grievance, receit
8. therefor, becaus, deft
9. rader, anceint, aerial
10. enormus, traveled, performed

B How many capital cities can you find in the wordsearch? Challenge a friend, and see who gets the most!

c	b	e	r	l	i	n	c	a	m	a	v
b	b	o	d	d	l	l	d	g	b	t	i
e	m	o	r	u	k	r	v	i	r	t	e
l	c	l	s	b	b	l	k	r	u	e	n
o	b	b	o	l	p	a	r	i	s	l	n
n	v	v	m	i	r	a	b	l	s	a	a
d	b	r	k	n	a	r	b	b	o	v	o
o	c	i	m	c	g	o	e	l	d	s	m
n	e	b	r	v	u	b	r	c	l	e	c
v	c	m	b	p	e	c	n	o	k	c	r
b	n	o	b	s	i	l	e	d	s	k	s
v	d	i	r	d	a	m	s	r	b	i	k

C Write the opposite of these words.

1. despair
2. occupied
3. invisible
4. innocent
5. import
6. found
7. south
8. often
9. exit
10. admit

78

Grammar

Contractions

> We often shorten words by running them together. An apostrophe (') is placed where a letter or letters have been left out.
> Example: If he can't go, you'll telephone me at nine o'clock.
>
> A list of common contractions:
>
> | | | | | | | | |
> |---|---|---|---|---|---|---|---|
> | He's | = he is | We've | = we have | Don't | = do not |
> | He'd | = he would | What's | = what is | We're | = we are |
> | He'll | = he will | Wasn't | = was not | She's | = she is |
> | I've | = I have | Isn't | = is not | It's | = it is |
> | You've | = you have | Can't | = cannot | | |
> | You're | = you are | Aren't | = are not | | |

A Rewrite the underlined words using apostrophes.

1. He is a good swimmer.
2. It is a lovely day.
3. I am very lucky to have such good friends.
4. I cannot go fishing today.
5. We have enjoyed our holiday.
6. You are welcome to come with us.
7. I will go to the shop for the messages.
8. The eel does not like to be touched.
9. He will regret his decision.
10. He should not have done that.

B Write the following sentences, using the shortened form of the words in bold type.

1. I **shall not** be able to finish my lessons this evening.
2. **Who will** come with me?
3. It **does not** matter if **it is** raining in the afternoon.
4. **I am** sure **she will** come with us on the cycling expedition.
5. **She is** the tallest girl in my class.
6. **That is** the boy **who is** playing in the tennis final.
7. **We are** going to visit the new museum as **it is** not far from here.
8. He **did not** know the correct answer.
9. Whenever **there is** a competition, she wins.
10. **It is** cold outside and **it is** raining.

C Write an apostrophe (') where the letter or letters have been omitted.

1. Dont ask her for the new record.
2. They havent yet finished their dinner.
3. If it isnt raining, well go to the park.
4. Theyll be late coming, so lets go.
5. Id like to go to the circus but I cant.

79

Writing

Newspapers

A Proofread the following article.

Nite of Terror

It shud have been the most spectacular selebration off the year. Instead, it was quiet frightening. The new year's eve street party on friday night became a riot, as chops were looted, kars were stolen and visitors were scared out of their mines. The chief of police, inspector burton, could not understand why some people began recking the city.

"It's far too early to explain, yet," was all she wud say.

At furst, everything seemed normal enuf. There was a happie atmosphere, as the countdown to midnite began. I taught I herd a loud crashing noise and wen i turned around, I realised that a stolen car had careered out of kontrol and smashed into a large departmint store window. the driver began running away from the scene and to my amazement, hundrets of people were climbin into the store and luting it. My Japanese friends were no loger smileing and I decided it was best to take them hom.

B Write an article for this headline.

Home Alone for Real

A child was found running from _____

C Write a television programme schedule for your newspaper, for one day. Include all your favourite programmes and what times they start.

80

Language

Abbreviations

> Sometimes words are not written in full. We often shorten or abbreviate them.
>
> Examples: (a) Captain Mary Connolly   Capt. M. Connolly
> (b) Professor Niamh Mary White   Prof. N.M. White
>
> Remember: (a) Full stops are used after abbreviations and initials.
> (b) Initials are written in capital letters.

A Insert the full stops and capital letters where necessary.

1. Next week a lecture will be given by Prof m b Foley.
2. Jas clancy and t Browne will present the television show.
3. Capt P H Green sat next to Mrs H mooney.
4. Prof M L clarke visited Capt ray Byrne.
5. Sir w s Fitzwilliam is our headmaster.
6. Yesterday, Miss k o'Neill died at 6 a.m.
7. My best friends are e McCarthy and j Murphy.
8. Lt Collins and Sgt Lynch went on the climbing expedition.
9. Next wed, Brown and co ltd are going to open a new supermarket.

B Write the following in abbreviated form.

1. Post Office
2. United Nations
3. Pay As You Earn
4. United States of America
5. Federal Bureau of Investigation

C What do these abbreviations mean?

1. P.T.O
2. Rev.
3. a.m.
4. P.S.
5. i.e.
6. m.p.h
7. N.B
8. E.U.
9. R.S.V.P.

D Write the following in abbreviated form.

Months	Abbreviations	Days	Abbreviations
January	Jan.	Sunday	Sun.
February	___	Monday	___
March	___	Tuesday	___
April	___	Wednesday	___
August	___	Thursday	___
September	___	Friday	___
October	___	Saturday	___
November	___		
December	___		

Note: The days and months of the year are written with capital letters. There are no abbreviations for May, June and July.

Reading

A Read the text.

The Submarine

The submarine works in a simple way. All submarines have large tanks which can be filled with water or air to make the ship submerge or rise. When the tanks are filled with water, the submarine becomes so heavy that it will sink. To stop the submarine from sinking all the way to the bottom of the sea, some water is pumped back out of the tanks. This will keep the submarine at the same depth. In order to come up again, the tanks are emptied of water and filled with air. The submarine is now light enough to rise to the surface.

The first submarine was built in 1803 by an American named Robert Fulton. It could only carry two people and its *propeller* had to be worked by hand. Yet Fulton knew that his machine could be of great use to any army at war. At that time, England and France were at war in Europe. So he travelled to France where he tried to sell his new invention to Napoleon. Even though he *succeeded* in blowing up a target with his submarine, the French were not interested. They thought it a most unfair way to fight a war. The *crafty* American then went to England, hoping to sell his submarine there. Two raids were made against French ships, but did not succeed. No one, at that time, was interested in Fulton's invention.

Today, of course, huge submarines travel through the waters of the world. Some of these ships are more than 200 metres in length, can move at a speed of 45 knots (88 kilometres per hour) and can dive to great depths. In 1958, a US submarine sailed under the ice to the North Pole. And in 1960 another US ship sailed around the world without once rising to the surface.

Activities

A **Answer these questions.**

1. How does a submarine rise?
2. How does a submarine sink?
3. What did Robert Fulton do in 1803?
4. Why did he travel to France?
5. Why were the French not interested in his invention?
6. How fast can today's submarines travel?
7. Where did a submarine sail to in 1958?
8. Can you name three of the world's oceans?
9. Try to make as many words as you can from "submarine".
10. Pretend you are a sailor on board a submarine. Write a paragraph about life on board your ship.

B **Look up the words in *italics* in your dictionary. Write an interesting sentence for each one.**

C **Summarise the story in your own words. Use about 10 sentences.**

D **Write has or have.**

1. I _____ a cat which _____ a sore paw.
2. The hen _____ a nest in the hay and so _____ the goose.
3. Goats _____ horns but chickens _____ not.
4. A turkey _____ two legs but a horse _____ four.
5. My cat _____ a white tail and her kittens _____ black tails.
6. The gander _____ a long neck but the cat _____ a short neck.
7. I _____ black hair but my sister _____ brown hair.
8. We have a Manx cat and she _____ no tail.
9. You _____ a dog but Mary _____ a cat.
10. The two of us _____ to work on the farm as our father _____ gone to the market.

83

Cloze

A Write the missing words.

most	insects	helping	about	small	treat	kept	good	attack	nest
eggs	let	different	burying	hatched	over	away	large		

Amazing Ants

With over 8,000 _____ species, ants must be one of the _____ successful of all the Earth's creatures. Unlike other _____ they will take very _____ care of their young – watching _____ them, feeding them, _____ them and even _____ them if they die. They may not be as kind to other ants however. Many ants go on "slave raids" where they _____ and carry away the _____ of other ants which are then _____ out to be worked as slaves. In any ant _____ you will find up to 500 species of other insects, many of which are simply _____ as pets for the amusement of their masters. The most startling thing of all _____ ants is the way they _____ the many greenfly they keep as prisoners. Firstly, the greenfly are locked _____ in pens, like cattle; the pens are _____ enough to _____ the ants in, but too _____ to allow the greenfly out!

B

than	actually	usually	creatures	winter	becoming	would	top
	under	prevents	for	layer	water		

Fortunately _____ animals in a pond in _____, the ice stays on the _____ of the _____. There is _____ sufficient water at the bottom of the pond in which the fish and other _____ can move _____ the ice. If the ice formed at the bottom, they _____ all freeze and die. The _____ of ice on top of the water _____ acts as a blanket and _____ the water at the bottom from _____ colder _____ it is.

84

Grammar

Conjunctions

> A conjunction is a joining word. It joins words, phrases or sentences together.
>
> Common conjunctions:
> and   as   but   so   although   unless   if   despite   either
> or   both   neither   nor   since   even   because

A **Underline the conjunctions.**

1. She will not go to the game unless she is driven there.
2. He speaks as if he knows everything.
3. We were locked out because we lost our keys.
4. I like coffee but I prefer tea.
5. We waited until my sister came home.
6. The dog lay down as though she was dead.
7. She started early so that she would finish in time.
8. You will not improve if you don't study.
9. Do not climb that tree or you might fall.
10. Although I tried, I did not win.

B **Write the missing conjunctions. Try not to use 'and' more than once.**

A new tunnel was planned _____ there was too much traffic for the only tunnel under the river. _____ it would be useful, it would be expensive _____ a toll would have to be paid by drivers. _____ local people protested about the toll, they were given special passes. Work was delayed for two months _____ there was a flood. _____ the flood went down _____ the workers soon made up for lost time.

C **Write these sentences, putting in conjunctions. Again do not overuse and or because.**

1. He was poor _____ honest.
2. The car was speeding _____ it went down the street.
3. He was presented with the prize _____ he deserved it.
4. _____ he goes with me _____ he stays at home.
5. _____ she _____ her friend went on holiday, it has been very quiet.
6. The monkey didn't jump _____ I threw him a nut.
7. She will not go _____ if you ask her.
8. He will not go to school _____ his father brings him.

85

Writing

Complete the Stories

A **Complete the following story.**

Last Saturday my friends and I went swimming in the "lake". We had tremendous fun in the cool water. Suddenly a cry for help went through the air. I rushed to the bank…

B **Complete the following story.**

"See how fast I can go," cried Mahmoud, as he raced past his admiring friends. He sped recklessly down the street. Daringly, he circled the roundabout. Suddenly…

C **Complete the following story.**

Femi wriggled into the sack. He was trembling with excitement. However, he was determined to win the race. The starter raised his arm and cried, "On your marks"…

D **Complete the following story.**

It was Mary's first ride on "Silver Spur". She leapt with joy into the saddle. A gentle touch of the reins, a word of encouragement, and horse and rider cantered across the field…

Language

> These words are spelled and pronounced alike, but differ in meaning.
> Example: Bat: an animal with wings.
>   Bat: a club to strike a ball.

A Write two meanings for each word. (Use a dictionary to help you if necessary.)

1. Bill
2. Bat
3. Blade
4. Box
5. Corn
6. Court
7. Crow
8. Flag
9. Game
10. Grave
11. Hail
12. Scale
13. Spring
14. Perch
15. Palm
16. Date
17. Draw
18. Crane
19. Club
20. Comb
21. Set
22. Graze

B Some words are pronounced alike but differ in meaning. Examine the clues and write the words.

1. An insect *(ant)*
   A close relation *(aunt)*
2. A male child _____
   A floating sign for ships _____
3. A female horse _____
   A head of a town _____
4. A bag of postal letters _____
   The opposite of female _____
5. A female sheep _____
   An evergreen tree _____
6. A strong odour _____
   An American coin _____
7. A valley _____
   A covering for the face _____
8. Used in a game _____
   To cry loudly _____
9. A sandy stretch of coastline _____
   A type of deciduous tree _____
10. A branch of a tree _____
    Part of a ship _____

C Write words that include the letters in the words given.

Cat	Air	Ale	Ear	Lip	Rat	Ore
Catalogue	Chair	Stale	Rear	Tulip	Crate	Core

87

Reading

A Read the story.

William Tell

Many years ago, Switzerland was conquered by an Austrian army. The Austrian governor of the little village of Altdorf was a wicked man named Gessler. In the village square he ordered a flagpole to be erected. The proud Gessler placed his feather hat on top of the pole. He wished to *humiliate* the Swiss people, by ordering them to kneel and bow before his hat.

William Tell, the best archer in Switzerland, happened to pass by the flagpole. He refused to bow to the governor's hat. As he was leaving the village with his son, the angry Gessler shouted, "Arrest that man."

Immediately the Austrian soldiers arrested William Tell. "People tell me you are a great marksman," jeered Gessler. "Let me see how good you are."

The cruel *tyrant* made William's young son, Jimmy, stand against an oak tree. On his head he placed an apple.

"You must split the apple in two, if you hope to go free," commanded Gessler.
Tell placed an arrow in his bow and took careful aim. The silent crowd watched anxiously. Suddenly the arrow whistled through the air. The apple split in two and the arrow buried itself in the tree. A great shout pierced the air. The people cheered with joy. William Tell's courage and skill had *foiled* the governor's cruel plan.

"I see you are carrying a second arrow," snarled Gessler.

"Yes," replied William, "and if my son had been injured, I intended the second arrow for your heart."

On hearing this, the Austrian ruler went wild with anger. "Soldiers, bind this man and take him across the lake to the castle *dungeons*."

William Tell was bound and thrown into a boat which was to carry him across the lake to the castle prison. His friends took his young son and hid him in a safe place.

While crossing the lake a terrible storm arose. William was an expert sailor and the soldiers *unbound* him and asked him to take the helm. In the twinkling of an eye, the clever oarsman steered the boat near a rocky ledge, sprang ashore and escaped into the mountains.

According to legend, when Gessler and his soldiers were searching the mountains for the prisoner, William saw the wicked governor, placed an arrow in his bow, took aim and fired. This time the arrow pierced the heart of Gessler, the tyrant. He fell from his horse, *mortally* wounded. At last the people of Altdorf had a new ruler and hero – William Tell.

Activities

A Answer these questions.

1. When and where did events in the story take place?
2. Who was Gessler?
3. How did he try to humiliate the Swiss people?
4. What was the name of William Tell's son?
5. How did Tell display his skills in archery?
6. What was the reason for the second arrow?
7. How did the tyrant Gessler die?
8. How do you know Tell was an expert sailor?
9. Why do you think the people of Altdorf chose Tell as their leader?
10. Write a list of your favourite five legends.

B Look up the words in *italics* in your dictionary. Write an interesting sentence for each one.

C William Tell was a famous Swiss archer. Write an interesting sentence about each of the following people.

1. Robin Hood
2. Huckleberry Finn
3. Goldilocks
4. Peter Pan
5. Cinderella
6. Rip Van Winkle

Cloze

Radar

A Write the missing words.

> arrival hit exactly mast second aircraft Moon safely
> measures screen thick back sound aerial picture ship's
> narrow solid waves travel

Radar

Radar helps to bring ships _____ to port and _____ to land, even in thick fog. It can warn of the approach of enemy aircraft and rockets. Radar has even travelled to the _____ and back.

You hear an echo when _____ waves bounce back from something solid. Radar works in the same way. Very short radio _____ are sent out in little bursts. When these waves hit something _____ they are bounced _____ again.

All radio waves _____ at the same speed – 297,600 km per _____ – so if we can measure how long it takes from the sending out of a wave burst to its _____ back again, we will know how far away the object is which the waves hit. A radar instrument _____ this in a very short time.

The radar _____ is at the top of the mast. The aerial goes round and as it does so it sends out wave bursts. When the waves _____ anything they are bounced back to the aerial.

The radar instrument on the ship's bridge shows the result on a _____ which is like a television screen.

The aerial sends out its invisible waves in a _____ beam, as a searchlight does. As the aerial on the _____ goes round and round, a _____ of the area round about the ship is "painted" on the screen.

The _____ navigator can therefore see on the screen _____ where the ship is, even if he/she is in _____ fog.

Grammar

Prepositions

> A preposition is a word which shows the relation between two other words.
> Example: The key is over the door.
> The mouse is under the box.

A Choose 10 prepositions and write them in a sentence of your own.

> about   above   across   after   against   along   amid   amidst   among   amongst   around   at   before   behind   below   beneath   beside   between   beyond   by   down   during   except   for   from   in   into   near   of   off   on   over   round   since   through   till   to   towards   under   underneath   until   unto   up   upon   with   within   without

B Write the sentences, choosing a suitable preposition.

> through   over   and   on   towards   at   into   down   of   in   by   to   through   against   with   under   up   from   for   between

1. The helicopter flew _____ the mountain and landed _____ the beach.
2. Last year I climbed _____ Mount Brandon _____ my best friend.
3. He went _____ the hardware shop and bought a tin _____ paint.
4. The library closed _____ an hour _____ one and two o'clock.
5. Jin-Ho jumped _____ the wall and ran _____ the gate.
6. We sheltered _____ a tree _____ the rain.
7. They sailed _____ the South Pacific _____ a large yacht.
8. Juventus played _____ AC Milan last Sunday and lost _____ one goal.
9. They escaped _____ the exit door and ran _____ the fire escape.
10. I will meet you _____ the shop _____ the railway station.

C Write sentences with the following phrases.

1. agreed to
2. went with
3. similar to
4. relied on
5. fought against
6. contrary to
7. different from
8. wrote to
9. aimed at
10. blamed for

D Write two prepositions that could be used after each verb.

1. walk
2. listen
3. argue
4. came
5. look
6. pick
7. stand
8. smash
9. talk

Writing

Conversations

A What do you say when:

1. You receive a gift?
2. You are introduced to a person?
3. You accidentally stand on a person's foot?
4. You meet an old friend in the street?
5. You ask for directions?
6. You go to a birthday party?
7. You apologise for doing something wrong?
8. You contradict a person?
9. Your uncle and aunt visit your house?
10. Your friend passes her examination?

B Complete the following conversation.

Ali: Hello, may I speak to Badra, please?

Badra: _____

Ali: Hello Badra! This is Ali speaking.

Badra: _____

Ali: Our class is going on a cycling tour next Sunday. Perhaps you would like to join us?

Badra: _____

Ali: Fine! I shall expect to meet you outside the Town Hall at nine o'clock.

Badra: _____

C You left a new coat on the bus. Imagine the conversation you would have with the clerk in the Lost Property Office.

Clerk: Hello! This is the Lost Property Office.
You: _____

Clerk: What was the number of the bus you were travelling on?
You: _____

Clerk: Where were you sitting on the bus?
You: _____

Clerk: Please give me a description of the coat.
You: _____

Clerk: Did you have anything in the pockets?
You: _____

Clerk: Yes, we have a coat here that fits that description. You may collect it any day between 9.00 a.m. and 6.00 p.m.
You: _____

Language

'Then' – Overused Word

A Write these sentences, using another word for 'then'.

> finally   eventually   next   later on   after that   subsequently
> shortly afterwards   presently   at last   almost immediately   soon afterwards

Mary carefully wrote the address on the envelope and placed the stamp on the right-hand corner. then she ran to the pillarbox at the corner of the street and dropped the letter into the box. then her letter was on its way to her Aunt Julia. then the postman arrived in the mail van and emptied the pillarbox. then the mail was brought to the Post Office where it was post-marked and sorted. then that evening all the airmail letters were placed in special sacks, and labelled "Airmail". then these sacks were carried to the main airport and placed aboard a Boeing jet – destination New York. then at Kennedy Airport a mail van was waiting as parcels were again sorted and placed in canvas bags for the different post offices in New York. then the following morning Mary's letter was delivered to her aunt's apartment. then it had reached its destination.

B Change the first letter of each word to form a new word. Then change the last letter of the new word to compose another new word.

		New Word	Second	New Word
Example	1.	BOOK	COOK	COOL
	2.	LIST	___IST	___IS___
	3.	KILL	___ILL	___IL___
	4.	COAT	___OAT	___OA___
	5.	HELL	___ELL	___EL___
	6.	PAIR	___AIR	___AI___
	7.	RACE	___ACE	___AC___
	8.	PEAR	___EAR	___EA___
	9.	BOOT	___OOT	___OO___
	10.	CELL	___ELL	___EL___

C Write **do** or **does**.

1. What _____ you _____ on your birthday?
2. I _____ not know how to make the plum pudding but my mother _____.
3. What _____ Dad have to _____ on Tuesday?
4. Why _____ he not _____ the painting with you?
5. She _____ not know how to _____ the cooking.
6. Jane _____ her best and she cannot _____ more.
7. She _____ need plenty of rest and so _____ you.
8. _____ clean the room as it _____ look very dirty and untidy.
9. I shall _____ the dusting and you will _____ the cleaning.
10. It _____ not matter now whether he _____ it or not.

Revision

Grammar

A Write the sentences, using suitable adverbs. Then finish each sentence.

> furiously   gracefully   powerfully   quietly   courageously   easily
> bravely   swiftly   superbly   carefully

1. She skated _____ around _____.
2. He sprinted _____ towards _____.
3. John swam _____ through _____.
4. The boxer fought _____ until _____.
5. The referee walked _____ across _____.
6. She played _____ for _____.
7. Abdul read _____ till _____.
8. Lin was _____ the best _____.
9. He wrestled _____ but _____.
10. The driver drove _____ along _____.

B Write the sentences using suitable verbs.

1. The wasp _____ (*stung, licked, pinched*) Mary on the neck.
2. The goat _____ (*pulled, butted, spiked*) Elizabeth with his horns.
3. The hedgehog _____ (*tickled, nibbled, prodded*) the dog with his spikes.
4. The Alsatian _____ (*chewed, bit, munched*) my sister on the hand.
5. The hen _____ (*pecked, gnawed, sniffed*) the little worm.
6. The jellyfish _____ (*gulped, snorted, stung*) the girl on the leg.
7. The crab _____ (*chewed, pinched, sucked*) me with his nippers.
8. The lion _____ (*poisoned, devoured, smothered*) the dead zebra.
9. The horse _____ (*trotted, nuzzled, patted*) its nose against my hand.
10. The little worm _____ (*walked, waddled, wriggled*) under the stone.

C Write the sentences and underline the nouns.

1. Pat and Kate went to the seaside.
2. Mongolia is a large country in Asia.
3. For many years, Marie Curie lived and worked in Paris.
4. The chain was made of gold.
5. The dog likes to eat meat and chew bones.
6. Last Friday we ate fish for dinner.
7. A spade is made of wood.
8. Tom uses a tractor when ploughing, but John uses a team of horses.
9. He managed to escape under cover of darkness.
10. Patagonia is a beautiful region in South America.

Language

'Got' – Overused Word

Got, Get, Getting
These words are used too often in conversation and writing. A more varied vocabulary is needed.

A Write the following sentences, replacing the underlined words with one of the words in the list.

suggested   improving   pass   lift   remove   awoke   prepared   bought
boarded   enjoy   reaches   rode   cycling   became   plunged
developed   decreasing   increasing   sorting   out

1. I got up early and got my breakfast.
2. John got on his bicycle, and succeeded in getting through the crowd.
3. They got the right ticket, but got on the wrong bus.
4. She will get a magnificent view when she gets to the top of the mountain.
5. get the top off the box, and get rid of the contents.
6. Our emigration figures are getting smaller, but our population is getting bigger.
7. Kim is getting on in his new school, and he hopes to get his examination.
8. My sister got impatient while she was arranging the flower display.
9. Anya has got the best way I know of getting around the problem.
10. After he got into the icy waters, he got a cramp in his right leg.

'Put' – avoid using this word in your writing. Choose more exciting and interesting words.

B Write the following sentences replacing the underlined words with one from the list.

increased   suppressed   annoyed   extinguished   tolerate   cancelled

1. She put off her visit to the dentist.
2. He was put off when the referee ordered him off the field.
3. The team manager cannot put up with such bad behaviour.
4. The government put up the price of petrol.
5. The army put down the prisoners' revolt.
6. When the rain started, she put out her cigarette.

95

Language

Silent Letters

Silent letters are letters that are used to spell a word but are not pronounced. Example: the 'b' in climb is silent.

A Underline the silent letters.

1. clim<u>b</u>
2. scene
3. sign
4. height
5. heir
6. knit
7. should
8. calf
9. solemn
10. psalm
11. empty
12. aisle
13. apostle
14. wren
15. doubt
16. abscess
17. knob
18. talk

B Write the word. Underline the silent letter.

1. A young sheep. — lam<u>b</u>
2. Someone who repairs pipes. — p
3. A grave or monument. — t
4. Used to arrange your hair. — c
5. An odour or smell. — s
6. Land surrounded by water. — i
7. A sailing boat. — y
8. A small bird. — w
9. The yellow of an egg. — y
10. A sacred song. — h
11. The opposite of "son". — d
12. The third season of the year. — a
13. A muscle in your lower leg. — c
14. Sixty minutes — h
15. To divide in two equal parts. — h
16. Sharp-bladed weapon. — s
17. A morsel of bread. — c
18. A garland of flowers. — w
19. A red berry fruit. — r
20. A tiny, winged insect. — g
21. The opposite of "native". — f
22. A prickly plant. — t
23. Joint in the leg. — k

96